Trouble in Glamour Town

S.R. MALLERY

Trouble in Glamour Town
By S. R. Mallery
Copyright © 2017 by S. R. Mallery
All rights reserved.

No part of this publication may be reproduced, stored in a retrieval system, or transmitted by any means electronic, mechanical, photocopying, recording or otherwise without the written permission of the author, except in the case of brief quotations embodied in critical articles and reviews.

This is a work of historical fiction. Names of real people, places, and film titles from the time are depicted along with fictitious characters. Imagined dialogues are loosely based on research, not documented speech.

Contact: https://www.srmallery.blog

ISBN-13: 978-1979566070
ISBN-10: 1979566070

DEDICATION

To my father, Jerome Ross, whose prolific body of television scripts has always been my source of inspiration, without my even knowing it—until now.

TABLE OF CONTENTS

ACKNOWLEDGMENTS i
PROLOGUE 1
CHAPTER ONE 3
CHAPTER TWO 12
CHAPTER THREE 24
CHAPTER FOUR 34
CHAPTER FIVE 42
CHAPTER SIX 49
CHAPTER SEVEN 65
CHAPTER EIGHT 76
CHAPTER NINE 88
CHAPTER TEN 100
CHAPTER ELEVEN 111
CHAPTER TWELVE 124
CHAPTER THIRTEEN 139
CHAPTER FOURTEEN 150
CHAPTER FIFTEEN 163
CHAPTER SIXTEEN 174
EPILOGUE 185
THANK YOU 191
ABOUT THE AUTHOR 192

OTHER BOOKS BY S.R. MALLERY

THE DOLAN GIRLS – In 1800's Nebraska, where ladies of the night, brutal outlaws, colorful land rushes, and Buffalo Bill's Wild West shows are the norm, can a whorehouse madam and her schoolmarm daughter both find true love?

UNEXPECTED GIFTS - Can we learn from our ancestors? Confused college student learns about life from her ancestors' journals, as she reads of their time during Vietnam, Woodstock, McCarthyism, the Great Depression, and their arrival on Ellis Island and fighting as Suffragists.

GENTEEL SECRETS - In 1861 America, can the love between a Confederate female spy and the Pinkerton detective hired to shadow her survive, or will their story become just another casualty of war?

SEWING CAN BE DANGEROUS AND OTHER SMALL THREADS - History, mystery, action, and romance are all rolled into one book in this 2016 Gold Medal winner of Reader's Favorite contest in Anthologies. Eleven short stories follow drug traffickers using hand-woven wallets, a U.S. slave sewing freedom codes into quilts, a cruise ship murder mystery, hiding Christian passports in Nazi Germany; a Salem Witchcraft quilt curse, the Triangle Shirtwaist Factory fire, and a 1967 Haight-Ashbury love affair gone horribly wrong.

TALES TO COUNT ON - Whether it's 500 words or 5,000, these stories, where sad meets bizarre and deception meets humor; where history meets revenge and magic collides with gothic, will remind you that in the end, nothing is ever what it seems.

.

ACKNOWLEDGMENTS

Over time I've learned a good editor is tantamount to having a loving and instructive parent, an attentive teacher, and a supportive mentor. In that regard, I completely depend on Patricia Zick, who keeps my creative thoughts forever grinding, my love of research applauded, and my prose, relentlessly examined. Thanks also to my *Trouble in Glamour Town* beta readers – Uvi Poznansky and Jacquie Biggar. Uvi, your early, eagle eye for details, consistency, and logic was so very helpful. Jacquie, your later fine-tooth combing, catches, and suggestions were insightful and much appreciated

PROLOGUE

*"It will take a bit of effort…a bit of sweat and perhaps…
a bit of blood."*
— From the 1922 movie, *Nosferatu*

January 4, 1926, 1:15 p.m.

IT WAS ANOTHER glorious day in Los Angeles. Sparkling like actress Theda Bara's bejeweled robe in the 1917 movie, *Cleopatra*, the Hollywood hills behind the man and his rifle glistened in the midday sun as each ray glanced off the small, jagged rocks. With his 1903 Springfield bolt-action sharpshooter locked tight against his shoulder, the assassin slowly rolled the scope ring around to set the precise distance. He knew from experience that with the wind factor leveled near zero, his chances were good for a clean hit.

For the third time, he peered through the lens. Fifty yards directly south of his position on the low-lying rooftop was Medford Studio's back lot. There, on the outdoor set, where a Bell & Howell 35mm camera had been set up on a wooden tripod, an agitated film director was busy barking orders through his giant megaphone, while all the actors remained frozen in their assigned positions.

Yet to the killer, none of that scenario was important. All he cared about was how his target stood off to one side, in perfect alignment with his scope view.

"Here we go, here we go," he muttered. He steadied himself against the roof edge and made sure the bolt was in the forward down position. With one eye pressed against the scope, he curled his index finger around the trigger and squeezed.

On the set, the director was still hollering his directions to the actors and crew when the shot rang out.

"Man down," the shooter said as human screams from below echoed up to him.

With a quick 'that's done' sigh of relief, the killer, still clutching his rifle, wiggled backward on his belly before he stood up out of sight of the ensuing chaos. A glance down at his shoes assured him the cloth swabs covering them were still in place. Then, his bag tucked under his arm, he hurried over to the outside ladder on the roof's back edge. From there, he deftly descended, grateful he had practiced this procedure at least once beforehand.

"Oh my God! Mr. Harris has been shot!" shrieked a nearby actress.

"Somebody get help!" screamed several others.

In a flash, a small crowd had surrounded the victim, who wore a leather World War I bombardier jacket, expensive trousers, and lay face down in his own blood. Underneath his balding head, bright red liquid fanned outward as two men attempted to turn him over to check his pulse.

Stunned murmurs fused with one or two muffled sobs. Someone sprinted into the main building, yelling over his shoulder that he would phone the police. Soon, the faint sound of sirens could be heard, growing louder and louder by the second until finally, the blare was so deafening outside Medford's front gate, people plugged their fingers in their ears.

Within minutes, the set swarmed with police—pushing, shoving, and steering people away from the man with a hole in his forehead: Chester Harris, the film's producer.

A detective grabbed the megaphone from the director and bellowed, "Folks, nobody leaves the set!" He paused for several seconds. "Everybody needs to stay put so we can get your information."

When two men sporting "coroner" labels turned over the corpse, the detective approached them, side-stepping a pool of blood.

"Yep. He's a goner, Detective Lozano," one of coroners said.

CHAPTER ONE

"There are girls, not specially beautiful, whom you could not lose in a crowd. There are other girls, apparently perfect in beauty, who seem to melt into insignificance."
— Mack Sennett, comedy film director

January 4, 1926, 1:35 p.m.

DETECTIVE FRANK LOZANO sighed. Swarthy, with a day-old stubble and broad shoulders, he reached into his cheap, oversized suit jacket and withdrew a small notepad and pencil. Logging in some notes, his mind rushed. *Three long-range homicides this year—all three cases, a single shot to the head. Same kind of hit, same feel.*

He adopted his signature tough cop position and started in.

"Folks," he called out in a deep, Brooklynese growl—this time without the cone-shaped device. "In case you didn't get it the first time, I'll say it again. We're gonna do some questioning. Nobody, but *nobody* leaves until you're cleared from the set. Got that?"

Motioning to his men, he signaled them to circulate throughout the set to ask each person some questions—the what-happened, name-address-telephone, and how-much-did-they-know-about-the-victim kind. After several minutes, pleased his fellow cops were actually making some headway, he stepped back and shaded his eyes against the sun. He scanned a group of pretty actresses off to one side. A good place to begin his own inquiries.

After ten interviews with the young women, he shook his head. These would-be starlets. Probably from all over the country, with their good-looking faces, fine, well-shaped gams, and ill-thought out pipe dreams. And where would they be in a couple of years? Most of them would either be gone or slaving away, doing God knows what, just to get a walk-on from these producers. And the studio heads? They weren't worth warm spit. It was hard enough to try and keep Los Angeles safe these days, but the movie studios, too? It just didn't seem—

In a flash, he caught sight of her across the way. Curly, auburn-colored hair, a cherubic mouth not even the Renaissance painters could match, and sparkling green, intelligent-looking eyes. Just watching her give comfort to a crying actress next to her, he felt a tiny tug at his heart. When a fellow officer began to interview her, Frank hot-footed over.

"Take a break, officer," he said. "I'll take this one for questioning."

The officer shrugged and disappeared. Standing close to her, Frank noticed she was trembling and twisting her hands together so tightly, it looked as if she were wringing out wet laundry. He glanced at her delicate neck, her shoulders, her small waist. *Stop it!*

He cleared his throat. "What's your name, miss?" He tried to keep his voice even, but it came out jagged.

"Rosie Paige," she said, her eyes wide.

He could smell her faint lavender toilet water. *Focus.* "Let's start with the basics, then, Miss Paige. What's your address and phone number?"

She told him, her voice lower in pitch than the other dames.

"The Highland Courts?" He whistled softly. "That's a nice complex. How come you're not at the Medford apartments on Fountain Avenue, like so many of you actresses who work at Medford Studios?"

"Medford did want me to stay there, but that wouldn't do. I'm with my mother."

Both a looker and loyal to family. He couldn't help himself. His hooded eyes drifted over to that mouth, that tempting kisser. *Enough!* "So, can you tell me anything about the victim?" he asked in a softer voice.

He had already learned through the grapevine the dead producer, Chester Harris, was never going to win a popularity contest. Numerous comments from other interviewees about his nastiness on set and his nasty dealings off set had Frank convinced this was not a crying-shame kind of loss. Still, he wanted to hear anything she had to say, wanted to watch those lips move—

hear those alto tones.

A new expression spread over her face. What was it? Fear-of-losing-one's job nervousness? "Don't worry, Miss Paige, I'd just like your honest opinion." He smiled.

Her handwringing stopped. "I didn't have much to do with him, but I've heard from some of the others he was not well-liked. Had some shady business dealings, too."

"Oh? And what's your role in this movie? Obviously, you're an actress."

The twitch of a smirk appeared on her lips. "Are you implying I'm empty-headed, detective?" Her rich voice held a hint of coyness.

He could feel his face warming. "No, no. Just that you're, well, pretty." He cleared his throat. "Like the other girls." He tried not to look more smitten than he felt. He opened his mouth, but paused at her new expression. She was looking past him, her eyes welling up.

"Eddie!" she cried and reached out one hand.

Whipping around, Frank watched a handsome, strapping young fellow bound over toward them.

"Who the hell is this?" the detective blurted out.

"My boyfriend."

As soon as Eddie joined her, they fell into a tight embrace. One quick kiss, and he was holding her and stroking her. "It's gonna be okay, it's gonna be okay," he murmured into her hair.

Startled by his own crushed reaction, Frank tried to steady himself. "I'll need your name and address, whoever you are."

Ignoring everything else, Eddie took a couple more seconds of comforting Rosie before facing the detective. "Eddie Willis is the name." He gave his address at a nearby rooming house.

"And what is it you do, Willis?"

"He's a jack of all trades," Rosie said. "You name it, he can do it." A tiny smile appeared.

Frank shook his head. *Damn, she's a goner for this guy.* "Willis, why don't you tell me instead of having your girlfriend do it."

Eddie sighed. "Like Miss Paige said, I do some carpentry, the occasional errand, make-up assistance when Mr. Lon Chaney needs me, and on this set, I was also a title card writer."

"What the hell is that?" Frank barked.

"It happens to be a very important job, detective." Rosie raised her voice.

"He writes the dialogue on cards for all the movie-goers."

The detective turned to Eddie. "You make up the dialogue?"

Eddie nodded. "Sometimes I do, yes."

For several moments, Frank became immersed in his notes, deliberately keeping them waiting. Finally, he looked up. "So, what was your relationship with the deceased?"

Eddie shifted and looked away.

The detective's pulse quickened. "Answer me. What was it?"

Just then, two men ambled by. One of them was attractive, well built, and clutched a camera tripod. The other was a skinny, slip of a man, dressed to the nines in a well-tailored suit. As he passed, Frank got a whiff of cologne.

"Boy, if anyone had a right to shoot that guy, you did, Eddie Willis!" the tripod carrier said.

Frank pointed to a tent nearby. "You two men, wait for me over there, *capish?*"

They both nodded, and once the detective saw them settled in the shade waiting for him, he turned back to Eddie, his eyes narrowed.

"Just what did that guy mean, Willis? Why would you want to shoot Harris, huh?"

"Everyone had a gripe with Chester Harris, not just Eddie. He…" Rosie started.

Without looking directly at the actress, Frank held up his hand toward her. "Willis," he continued, "you're gonna tell me now, or you're gonna tell me later. But you sure as hell are gonna tell me."

Eddie shrugged. "It wasn't that bad. A while back, Harris was shabby to a friend of mine. Got him fired for no good reason, so I went to Harris' office to complain. He didn't like that. We had a few words. It's as simple as that. But we both got past it, and in fact, recently, all of a sudden, the producer started asking me to run errands for him."

Frank's eyes slit even tighter. "So, you once had words, and he was a producer, right?"

Rosie and Eddie stared at him.

"Harris was a big shot producer," Frank continued, "so compared to him, you were low man on the totem pole. How come he didn't just fire you? You know, tell you to go chase yourself." He quickly looked at Rosie. "Sorry, Miss Paige."

"I told you I mostly work with Lon Chaney," Eddie said. "He has some clout. He backed me up at the time."

"Lon Chaney, *The Hunchback of Notre Dame* actor and famous makeup artist, Lon Chaney? Lucky you," Frank muttered, and opened up his notepad again.

"Detective, can I please take Miss Paige home? I think she's had enough for the day, don't you?" Eddie looked around. "I see other people have gotten cleared from the set."

Frank grimaced. He knew he couldn't hold her. "All right."

Arms locked, the couple walked away.

"Expect a visit from me, Willis. Soon," Frank yelled to their backs.

Rosie turned around and nodded as they walked away. Eddie did not.

There's trouble. He lit a cigarette. The smoke swirled up around him as he watched them for several beats before they both disappeared into the main Medford building. He then strolled over to the nearby tent, his pencil and pad at the ready.

The tripod man was his first focus. "Your name and address?" he asked.

"Pete Roberts." The good-looking fellow filled in the rest for the detective.

"Let me see. Your job is cameraman?"

"Good guess, detective," the cologne guy said with a twisted smile.

Frank shot him a dirty look.

"Anyway," Frank went on, "Mr. Roberts, tell me why you think Eddie Willis had a motive in killing the victim, Mr. Harris."

The policeman wasn't prepared for the litany of rapid-fire accusations from Pete Roberts.

"Willis was always trying to be the he-man on the set. You know, the one who was helpful to everyone, running errands for Chaney and recently Harris. Mr. Handsome, Mr. Good Guy. He especially tried to be helpful with the actresses."

"You mean that Rosie Paige, don't you?" The one with the fine suit interjected.

"Rosie Paige?" Frank leaned in.

"Yeah, she's Eddie's girl, and you don't like that, do you, Pete?" the thin loudmouth sneered. Frank shook his head. *Guess I'm not the only one interested in this Rosie.* He scrutinized Pete's red face. "Do you have any concrete reason why you think Willis would do it, other than the obvious?"

"The obvious, detective?" Pete cocked his head.

"You wanting to put someone away who's seeing the girl you're interested in." Frank almost felt sympathy for the guy. *Can't blame him, though.* Putting away Willis and freeing up Rosie was appealing.

"He was away from the set when the shot came," Pete said.

"Yeah," the slender troublemaker agreed, his eyes a little too intense for Frank's liking.

Frank swatted his hand toward Pete with a you-can-go-now gesture and concentrated on the Cologne Man. "And your name and address?"

"The name's Henry Blake, and you can get all my particulars from the studio office. I was assistant to Chester Harris."

There was something about Blake he couldn't quite put his finger on. Bitterness? Anger? Hurt? He figured he would have to question this one at the police station. And sometime soon. Unlike the cameraman who just seemed to have a beef with Eddie because of Rosie, Henry Blake was closer to the victim. All Frank's instincts told him the man smelled fishy.

"I would assume you knew the victim pretty well, being his assistant and all, right?"

Henry avoided Frank's stare. "As much as anyone. We weren't very close. I just did whatever he needed, nothing more, nothing less."

"Did you know him enough to guess who might wanna do him in?"

This time there was only a headshake.

"A man of few words when it comes to yourself, huh?"

"Don't know what else to add, detective, that's all."

Frank stepped back a pace and put his scribbling away. "Just don't leave town, Mr. Blake. I'll be calling you for further questioning." He searched for signs of worry or fear on Blake's face, but found none. *This guy sure has a poker face.* He motioned the man away.

Far up into the Hollywood Hills, Henry Blake's modest Spanish villa was shrouded in English ivy. A European-style courtyard, furnished with a brick walkway, a four-leaf-clover shaped fountain tiled with Mexican motifs, and pot after decorated pot of Cacti was his haven, his sanctuary, his place where his ex-lover and he had spent many a night—and early morning—together. There, they didn't have to answer to the world at large. A world that would react, just seeing them together.

Exhausted from hiding his real emotions in front of that gumshoe detective, all he wanted to do now was lie back and relax. He should have known better. Closing his eyes, the scene from over a month ago floated through his brain. Without warning, he could feel the tears burn behind his eyelids.

"Damn him," Blake whispered and leaned back to let images from that evening invade his brain.

He remembered how the air, so thick earlier that day, had diffused into a fine, balmy summer's night. Perfect for yet another one of Julian Eltinge's clandestine parties. Hailed as a good actor on stage, vaudeville, and screen, Julian, a local icon, was also considered by many to be a brilliant female impersonator. Fiercely masculine in public—rumor had it he had bashed in the heads of a couple of set stagehands for just snickering at his personal proclivities—his private life was a different matter altogether. He had his beautiful Villa Capistrano, nestled high up in the hills of Silver Lake, and it was there that Eltinge could do whatever he damn well pleased.

The understated mansion sported a wrap-around balcony, with Romanesque columns and archways, wicker chairs, and potted palm fronds. At night, guests would gather there to chat about the vicissitudes of the film business and simultaneously, meet up and go home with partners who otherwise would be tagged as forbidden fruit.

Chester Harris had always been welcomed there, and, as he told Henry, he enjoyed every inch of the place. It was his getaway from a wife he wasn't at all interested in sexually and a place where he got to meet handsome young studs in the industry. It was also where he and Henry Blake first met.

Their yearlong affair had been passionate and consistently turbulent. And in time, Henry could tell that working together so closely on sets was beginning to take its toll on his older lover. The young assistant instinctively sensed that Chester might be feeling hemmed in, and maybe even bored. Henry had mulled over having a discussion with the producer, but never had the chance. So, it wasn't a complete surprise when it came to a head that summer's night up at Eltinge's. In fact, as soon as Henry appeared at Harris' side, he knew something ominous was about to play out. It did.

"Why don't you get your own conversations going for once?" Harris barked in a harsh, searing voice.

Stunned at such a public outburst, Henry watched Harris' gloating face as if in slow motion. He knew he was in trouble. "Chester, are you feeling all right?" His voice wobbled.

"Never been better in my life. Now, scat!"

The producer's grin felt like a knife stab. As Henry's humiliation increased, so did the attack.

"And by the way," Harris added, "the next time you ask the actors on the set to get in their places, I expect you not to do it in such a slapdash, amateurish way. In short, you're no good to anyone, Henry."

That was the nail on the coffin. Henry turned to leave, but not before swinging back toward his former lover. "Don't think I won't get you for this, Chester. Just you wait."

By the time Henry reached his home that night, he had softened, hopeful that they would make up, as they had done numerous times before. But it was not to be. After the insufferable treatment by Harris at the party, the very next day Henry had to endure two things on the set. First, there was a complete shunning of him by his ex-lover, without so much as a glance in his direction. Second, Harris asked Eddie Willis, of all people, to run his errands. All the things he had always asked Henry to do for him—getting coffee and picking up things Harris might leave in his office.

Two more weeks of that, and Henry knew he was going to get his revenge. After all, he was aware of his older lover's deep ties with the mob and the City Hall Gang and how fast and loose he played it with local gamblers and bootleggers with no thought of consequences.

Now, lying on his chaise lounge, Henry also drifted back to the conversation he had had with that special person who was going to help him get some of that revenge. All he had to do was cough up information about Chester, his life, and where he was going to be at all times of the day. Or night. The rest would be out of his hands.

For Frank, it felt like the longest drawn-out day he'd experienced in ages. Copious notes aside, he found the entire film industry was filled with a batch of deadbeats with steady bank accounts. Working hard on sets? *Give me a break.* How about getting down in the dirt and soot like his old man had to do as he fixed the filthy New York subway system? Or his grandfather, his back broken from farming on the Jersey shores? Or even himself, tracking down criminals, gore and all, while at the end of the day getting the bums' rush from his higher-ups for all his trouble.

He realized Harris was not someone he would have ever known, much less cared about. And as for the helpful, but jealous cameraman, Pete Roberts? Probably a waste of time. But Henry Blake was a different matter. Suspect written all over him—with a definite need for a much closer look. And Eddie Willis? There, Frank stalled. Eddie was a suspect all right, but things with him were, well, complicated, because of—

That Rosie girl. Now she was worth something, no doubt about it. Not like the other shallow, inarticulate tomatoes he'd interviewed today. *Wonder how her day was ending?* The unfamiliar splash of concern bubbling up inside him took him by surprise and made him want to find out more about her. Much more.

CHAPTER TWO

"My mother and I could always look out the same window without ever seeing the same thing."
— Gloria Swanson, actress

**January 4, 1926
AFTER the Harris Shooting
Evening**

OUTSIDE MEDFORD STUDIOS' front gate, the sun was already inching downward. The warm glow from streetlights reflecting off buildings, automobiles, and streetcars passing by had rendered the sky hazy, almost mystical. Once Eddie had opened the passenger door on his 1920 Model T, Rosie was grateful for how gentle he was in helping her inside. And grateful that he took the time to make sure she was comfortable before he walked around to the driver's seat to slide in next to her. Again, she could feel his eyes on her as she lay her head flat against the seatback. Her lips started to tremble, and tears cascaded down her cheeks, lingering on her chin for only a second before they dripped off onto her jacket.

He snuggled close enough to stroke her hair. "Rosie, sweetheart, you've been balled up all day. Why don't you try to doze a bit while I get this thing started and drive you home?"

"I don't know if I'll ever sleep again," she muttered. A slow, two-handed swipe of both eyes left her cheeks streaked with mascara.

Cupping one large hand over her small, delicate one, he gave it a double squeeze before returning to business. He set the car in neutral, pushed the half throttle in place, then retarded the spark. After another exit from the car, he strode around to the Ford's front end, and with a hard, short jerk, turned the crank. When the motor sputtered and coughed, he returned to his seat, put the car in forward gear and rumbled off.

As they drove through the Hollywood streets and jiggled over railroad trolley tracks, Rosie's mind drifted back to that fateful trip from Omaha two years earlier. Soon, the Model T's rickety movements melded into her memories of the Baltimore & Ohio train jostling its way out to Los Angeles. Back, back her brain went, to that morning on the Omaha platform, where her mama, Beatrice, stood beaming, stoked by Hollywood's allure.

Amidst "all aboard" calls, the whish of air pumps, the blast of steam dispensing a film of moisture everywhere, her ambitious mother pointed to a metal sign just outside the engineer's box.

"Look what the sign says, Rosie." Her mother's grin turned into a hearty laugh. It was the most hopeful sound Rosie had heard from her mother in years. "In God We Trust. Kind of funny having that placed there, where the engineers have to cling onto the walkways while the train is moving. You know, I've got a feeling this trip is going to be our 'In God We Trust' time. What do you think, Rosie?"

Rosie stared back blankly. What difference did it make what she thought? According to her mother, they were off to Glamour Town for "fame and fortune," and that was the end of it.

Jiggle-jiggle-bump went Eddie's car, sending her memories back to the train journey itself. It was an exhausting ride that had stretched across the vast prairies of Kansas, the burbling streams of Montana, and the jagged mountains of New Mexico and Arizona. She could still hear her mother talking endlessly about how her beautiful Rosie was going to be a star and take them to heights they had never known before. There would be major motion picture deals through Metro Goldwyn Mayer perhaps, RKO, or Medford Studios. Maybe she'd be the next Mary Pickford or work beside the likes of Charlie Chaplin. Rudolph Valentino would dance the tango with her, and Douglas Fairbanks would leap over walls to rescue her from danger on outdoor movie sets. Anything could happen.

"This is Hollywood, the city of second chances," was her mama's nonstop motto.

Jiggle-jiggle the car continued. Still in a half-awake, half-asleep trance, Rosie shifted back to how hungry she had been when they finally arrived at the Los Angeles train station at six o'clock in the evening. Desperate to fill her tummy, she had pointed to her open mouth and rubbed her stomach. But Beatrice wouldn't hear of it.

Jiggle-jiggle. Beatrice's voice still floated in and out.

"We were darn lucky to get into the Highland Courts through my cousin. We can always eat later. Lodgings don't come so easy. I'm not gonna risk any problems as soon as we're here, thank you very much."

Rosie had turned away from her mother and toward the palm tree-lined street.

"Can't even get nourishment," she muttered.

Beatrice had held up a finger. "And don't start any of your mumblings, young lady. I can hear you, you know."

By the time Rosie slowly rotated around to face her mother, she caught Beatrice's signature stance: arms cross-locked against her chest, legs rooted to the ground.

Jiggle-jiggle. Stop. At a cross section, the motor's *putt-putt-tick, putt-putt-tick* pushed her mind back again. Back to her first arrival at the Highland Courts. Back to their superintendent, Walt Madison.

Although silver-haired, his arms were still muscular. Rosie figured he was probably strong enough to lift heavy furniture without getting a heart attack. Despite all his wrinkles, his slate blue eyes remained clear, alert, with the look of hard-boiled, seen-it-all-before experience.

"You here to be a movie star?" had been his first words to her.

That had instantly made Beatrice laugh and Rosie sigh. Another ally for her mother's ambitions, she figured at the time, and in some ways, that had turned out to be true.

Jiggle-jiggle. Stop.

"Rosie, Rosie, we're here," Eddie said, gently shaking her.

Her eyelids slowly rolled open. "Already?" Her voice came to her as if in a fog.

Twenty yards from the curb, Highland Courts was dark, save for the one electric light bulb illuminating the front curved archway. Past the rounded portal lay the small grass and cobble-stoned courtyard, with Spanish bungalows on either side, each one with its own concrete stoop. In front of the complex stood an elderly man and a middle-aged woman.

"There they are," Eddie said. She noticed his mouth had shifted into a frown.

"Eddie, I don't know what my mother has against you, I really don't," she said softly.

He shrugged. "Don't you? She thinks anyone who's not a famous actor or a high roller producer is not good enough for you. And Walt? He'll back your mother to the ends of the earth."

"Yeah, you're probably right." But she knew for her mother, it was much more than that. As Beatrice and Walt were fast making their way over, she sighed loudly.

"We gotta face them," she said. Eddie got out of the car and started to come over to her door, but Walt beat him to it, his eyebrows drawn together.

"Where have you been with her?" Walt asked Eddie. "Beatrice told me Rosie was due off the set by mid-afternoon. Her mother has been worried sick."

Rosie placed her hand on their friend's arm. "Walt, it's not Eddie's fault."

"Yeah, there's more to it, Walt," Eddie said. He turned to Beatrice. "Mrs. Paige, something happened on the set today. You'll probably read all about it in the papers tomorrow morning for certain."

"What?" Beatrice's lips quivered as she put her arm around her daughter.

"Remember, Mama, I was assigned to that outdoor set from the movie Mr. Harris was producing," Rosie said.

Beatrice nodded. "Yeah, they made me stay up all night for it to finish that one costume."

"Yes. So, there we were, in the back lot when—"

"You were there, too, right?" Walt asked Eddie.

"No, actually, I wasn't," Eddie said.

Walt turned toward Rosie. "Go on, you tell it, Rosie. What happened?"

"She's trying to tell you," Eddie began, but stopped when Rosie gave him a frown.

Feeling like a limp rag by this time, Rosie could barely see straight. "Someone shot Mr. Harris," she said, welling up all over again.

Beatrice let out a choked moan. "Dear God."

"How did it happen?" Walt asked. "Do they know who did it?"

"Mrs. Paige, Walt, see how pale she looks," Eddie said. "And look at those dark circles under her eyes. She needs to get some sleep."

"Yes," Rosie said dully.

Beatrice made clucking noises as she took her daughter by the arm and guided her toward the front door. Just as they reached it, Rosie suddenly turned around.

"Thanks, Eddie," she said with as much energy as she could muster. "See you tomorrow?"

Eddie took a step forward, then stopped. Beatrice's lips were pressed tight, and her faithful Walt had placed himself in front of the apartment complex with his arms crossed.

"Good night, Rosie. Tomorrow it is," Eddie called back. After a small, weak wave from Rosie, he got back into his car, set his essentials, exited to crank the starter, slid back inside and drove off, not once looking back.

By ten o'clock, with Rosie safely inside, Walt and Beatrice sat on the front stoop, smoking cigarettes and conversing in low tones.

"Wonder what really happened." Walt squinted, as a cloud of smoke drifted up toward his eyes.

Beatrice sighed. "We'll find out the details tomorrow. As much as I hate to admit it, Eddie was right. Rosie needed to get some sleep. She looked awful."

"I suppose. I'm just glad she's home, safe."

A smile crept over her face. "You're always there for us, Walt."

He gave her the flicker of a wink. "I may not know from nothing, but I do know this: you and Rosie-Posey can always count on me."

"Yes, of course we do. Don't know what we'd have done without you these past two years."

Her eyes moistening, she began to rub each finger of her left hand with the fingers from her right. She stroked, massaged, and pulled at each one while Walt watched.

"Bea, what are you doing?"

As if awakened from a trance, Beatrice looked down at her hands and sighed. "Oh, dear, old habits, Walt. I used to rub lotion on my fingers after a long day of sewing. Rosie says I do it now when I'm…"

"Stressed?" he asked softly.

She nodded. The silence encircled them for a good ten seconds before she spoke again.

"You going to see your friend in the hospital this Saturday?"

He blinked. "Yeah, sure. Like I always do."

"You're a good man, Walt Madison," she said simply and got up. "Time for beddy-bye."

He stood up as well. "See you both in the morning." A quick peck on her cheek, and he ambled away.

That night, Rosie had her dream again—the recurring one that had secretly plagued her ever since her father had deserted them. Even though she had discussed it with Eddie, and he had told her how dreams could connect the dots, still, whenever it came to her it was unsettling, haunting even. The only thing she could count on was it always starred the same lead actress.

Her five-year-old hand crushed into a fist, the little girl pounds on the gray door with the rusty bronze knob. Behind her, sirens are wailing, in front of her is silence, with no response from within.

"Anybody here?" the little girl calls out.

No answer, just the sirens growing louder, more piercing.

Now she sees a swirl of flashing lights spotting the door in front of her with snowdrops of white. The girl flips around. "Leave me alone!" she screams at a faceless man coming toward her.

"But I'm here to help you," he replies, then disappears.

The little girl spins around toward the door and knocks again. This time, the door opens a crack.

"A-hah!" she cries in delight.

After several seconds, the door is as opened as it first was—hardly at all. Frustration makes the child strong, bold. With all her might, she pushes the heavy door and steps inside, where it is dark, save for a single ray of light escaping from the next room. An eerie sound penetrates the air, unlike anything she has ever heard. Step-by-step, tip-toe by tip-toe, the girl maneuvers through the darkness into the semi-lit room. There, surrounded by shadows, a man is sitting on a chair, his back to her. A standing lamp is next to him, shining down a smoky glow all around his form.

"Who are you? Can you help me?" asks the girl with a quaver.

She can hear the person stir, and when he rises, he is tall, broad, and holding something in his hand.

"Are you the one who's here to help me?" she whispers.

Excited to see who her savior is, she waits for him to turn around. He turns to face her.

He has no face, but he's holding a rifle, and it's aimed toward her.

This time, the chilling dream made her bolt upright, hugging herself, her teeth chattering. It also, within seconds, had her flashing back to times long before. Back to vivid memories of sitting on her father's lap with his strong, protective arms encasing her better than any blanket ever could. That image had always stayed with her. Even throughout her parents' increasing arguments over the smell of other ladies' perfumes on her papa's clothing. Even when he'd say more and more frequently, "Be a good girl, Rosie, and get off me. Papa's gotta go out now." Even when she thought she saw him kissing a woman outside their house late one night.

Then abruptly, he was no longer in their lives at all. In the wake of his exit, her protective instincts were strong, and at eight years old, she sensed her mama's needs had to be met before her own. Beatrice's mood swings and crying jags scared her, and nothing was worth being around that. Then Rosie made a discovery: She could lessen her mama's intense moods considerably by being overly concerned and utterly compliant.

That revelation came at a price. All too quickly, she brushed aside her own friends, her own fun times, and many of the things she had enjoyed. Except for animals, that is. Her mother couldn't take that away from her. The stronger Beatrice's bitterness became, the more Rosie craved rescuing and holding animals whenever she got a chance. People started commenting on how the neighborhood cats and dogs gravitated to her like magic whenever she came near them, and to her own delight, when she would pick them up and hold them close, it was like being enfolded in her father's arms all over again.

"Why you love those mangy animals so much is beyond me," Beatrice would mutter whenever that happened.

But this was one thing Rosie would not give up, no matter what her mother said, no matter how much she let her contempt for these furry "creatures" come out. Time turned out to be Rosie's friend. Slowly but surely, Beatrice's comments grew less stringent and simply faded into an occasional grimace.

In bed, still shaken from her frightening dream, Rosie took several deep breaths and attempted to imagine pleasant thoughts. But a sudden scratching at the door, along with a tiny yip, brought more relaxation than any vision could ever do. She leapt out of bed and opening it up, looked down at both her dog, Patches, and her cat, Ginger, sitting side by side, waiting for her.

With a small giggle, she stage-whispered, "Come on, guys, let's go back to bed."

Instantly, all three of them were on top of her covers for a good cuddle, with plenty of tail wagging and cat paw-kneading. Harris' murder and loaded rifles were gratefully shoved aside.

The night before, after Walt had left, a nervous Beatrice went inside, made herself a cup of tea, then settled down on the sofa. She tilted her head back against the cushions, and trying to push thoughts of what could have happened on the set earlier with Rosie there, let her mind revisit her early days at Medford Studios.

She realized just how fortunate she was to get a seamstress job in the first place. The pay was better than what the other studios had to offer, and when she was able to bring Rosie onboard, things seemed perfect. Or so she thought. Reality soon sifted in. The pay was decent, but the hours were interminable. Leaving at the crack of dawn and returning home far too late became her routine. As a result, Rosie would have to either heat up food from the night before or scrounge around in the pantry to come up with something, anything, for the both of them. And with a hungry Walt often dropping by, Beatrice knew she had to make sure there was always enough available in the larder for their male company.

Unfortunately, at this "coveted" job in the costume department, amongst luscious, European fabrics, fine French lace, and miniature gems, she soon saw a side of Hollywood that was far from ideal. During the daily parade of dress fittings, she realized she had become invisible to the actresses coming in—those beautiful, desperate girls who chatted up a storm while Beatrice blithely measured, cut, pinned, and hemmed their clothing. Twelve hours a day, six days a week, the one relief was she knew that her own Rosie would not be like these shallow girls with their loose morals. Nor would she be tempted to get into cocaine, like the famous wise cracking "Queen of Comedy" Mabel Normand had, according to all the studio scuttlebutt. No, her daughter was going to be better than all that. She was going to be a star, and an untarnished one at that.

Lying back on the sofa, Beatrice remembered a conversation that had taken place just two months before.

It had started with a casual comment from one of the girls there for a fitting.

"I love this costume room. It's such a hen coop," a pretty, big-busted girl had said.

"A hen coop?" Beatrice had asked.

"Yeah, you know, like a beauty parlor where we're all free to talk."

"Speaking of free talk, did you hear what happened to Lana Freemont?" another girl asked. She was wearing a cream-colored, knee-high slip and paid no attention to Beatrice expertly wrapping a measuring-tape around her bust, waist, and hips.

As soon as the seamstress wrote down the girl's measurements in a little book, she moved on to the other girl, dressed in a Louis XVI period gown.

"No, do tell," the French Court girl said, breathless with excitement as Beatrice aggressively pinned back the gown's waist to enhance the actress' hourglass figure.

The slip girl turned hush-hush. "I heard from a friend of hers that Lana was invited by her agent to some big, fancy Hollywood party, way up on Mulholland Drive, in the middle of nowhere."

"And?" The French Court girl leaned in and dramatically cupped her ear.

Beatrice shook her head at the girl's showiness. Still, she paused unconsciously to hear what would come next.

"She told me it was packed with older men with their young girls. You know, men that weren't just Hollywood fellas. Men that looked as crooked as a bent fender, if you get what I mean."

"Bootleggers? Yeah, I heard these days those kinda men are called, "Sugar Daddys." Sorry, go on,'" Frenchy said.

"And the bank wasn't closed, if ya know what I mean. There was more than enough kissin' and pettin' going on."

"Oh yeah? More details!" exclaimed another.

"Well. According to Lana's friend, there was lots of "giggle water." Large tubs of champagne came with constant petting on couches and even more stuff upstairs in bedrooms. And drugs? Why, they were everywhere Lana looked. Containers of heroin and cocaine were sitting right smack dab in plain sight on the piano. Besides that, there was a huge swimming pool where people were naked in the water, doing, you know what."

Beatrice snorted contemptuously while the French Court girl laughed. "Sounds like fun! Ouch!" she called out. Looking down at Beatrice who was on her knees below her, the pin in the seamstress' mouth had just pricked the actress' bare leg. "Watch those pins, Mrs. Paige!"

"Shall I go on?" the cream-color slip girl asked, tapping one foot.

Frenchy, the other gal, and Beatrice all nodded.

"There was bad liquor there, too. Some real wood alcohol, if you know what I mean. And Lana was forced to drink some."

"*Forced* to?" Beatrice couldn't help herself.

"Yeah, her agent had deserted her, and two big fat men grabbed her and took her upstairs to a bedroom. Threw her on the bed, just like they say Fatty Arbuckle did with Virginia Rapp. Then they tied her to the bedposts and forced gin down her throat. That was before they raped her."

The room got conspicuously quiet.

"Lana ended up in the hospital room that night, to get her stomach pumped and take care of, well…"

"Well?" Beatrice asked.

"A lot of internal bleeding. They say she'll never act again."

Exhausted from her thoughts, Beatrice got up from the couch and shuffled off to bed. Yet she didn't fall asleep instantly. First, she murmured the prayer she always whispered each night: *Lord, let us be healthy and well in our lives. And if you see fit, let Rosie rise above the studio girls and be rich and famous, that's all I'm asking.*

That was her usual cue to forget all else and dive straight into unconsciousness. But tonight, her mind stretched to another thought: *What in the world really happened on that set?*

December 4, 1925
A Month BEFORE the Harris Shooting

This was twenty-year-old Alonzo Casale's big chance. Raised in a Brooklyn orphanage, introduced to and miraculously accepted into the Los Angeles' Ardizzone gang through his cousin, Tony, he took his first Hollywood assignment seriously. No fooling around. This was it, his proving ground.

Turns out, Tony was Ardizzone's right hand man, and when the kingpin gave the go-ahead to try out his young cousin, Alonzo, Tony was succinct with his orders.

"We need to lean on this Harris guy, Alonzo. He's at least two months behind in his payments, and frankly, the boss ain't too happy about it. The usual guys for this kinda thing are otherwise occupied, so I guess it'll be you, kid, with Ardizzone's blessing. So, don't let me down." He let that resonate. "Now, what you got to threaten him with? What's your piece?"

Nodding solemnly, Alonzo showed his weapon of choice, a .38 M&P revolver. He had bought it off an ex-cop, behind one of those "special" Long Beach warehouses, the kind that contained boxes of illegal booze.

Tony also told him that the meeting with Harris had already been set up by someone named Charles Crawford. "And by the way, don't ever be late, 'cause neither Crawford nor Ardizzone take kindly to that," his cousin added.

That was fine with Alonzo. He'd be there on time, all right.

Or so he thought. But first off, he had trouble starting his neighbor's loaner Tin Can Lizzy. Then, when he got lost halfway down to the small beach town, he realized he must have read the directions wrong. Finally, by the time he arrived, Harris wasn't even there. Sweating like a pig, Alonzo was all set to make a full confession to Tony, Ardizzone, or anyone who would listen. Then pray there was a God. Memories of being beaten and teased at the orphanage reared their ugly head, until he talked to another one of Ardizzone's men who had also been stationed at the warehouse. Turns out Harris had never even showed up.

So, Alonzo missed a possible beating or worse that day. Not told about the new boy's tardiness, Ardizzone seemed to focus on the fact that his new recruitment had come to do his duty, even if that rich, no good, coward Hollywood producer Harris had not. So, in order for Alonzo to use his gun with professional acumen, Ardizzone suggested the young recruit learn how to shoot properly as soon as possible, with Tony as his teacher.

On their first day out together a mile or two beyond the orange groves of San Fernando Valley, his cousin Tony and one other Ardizzone employee had discovered something unexpected. Alonzo was a damn good shot. He was so good, it quickly went up the rumor mill to Ardizzone himself, and before long, Tony was told by the Big Boss, to have his cousin, Alonzo, practice with a rifle, "because maybe I got a special job for him to do."

CHAPTER THREE

*"I want them brought in dead, not alive,
and I will reprimand any officer who shows
the least mercy to a criminal."*
— Newly appointed Chief of Los Angeles Police,
James E. Davis

**January 5, 1926
One Day AFTER the Harris Shooting
9:05 a.m.**

AS SOON AS Frank Lozano stepped into the main room of the Hollywood police station on Cahuenga Avenue, the chaotic hum of voices hit him like a smack in the face. Used to negligence and disinterest, he was amazed to see the room erupting with activity. The two secretaries were frantically hopping about like marionettes on strings, their usual dangling cigarettes abandoned. They were taking countless phone messages, opening up and slamming shut the wooden filing cabinet drawers, and each time they finished a task for one detective, another gumshoe would bark orders at them to do something else for him.

When they saw Frank, they both darted over to him.

"Detective Lozano, any more word on this Harris case?" one of them asked. Her blouse was stained with sweat around her armpits.

"We're going crazy in here," the other woman said. "No one seems to know anything." Frank sighed. In spite of the frenetic pace in the room, he knew in the end, it would be just another frustrating day in an incompetent unit.

"Ladies, ladies. Hold your horses. Captain Billings has asked me to help him get a meeting going, and that's what I aim to do."

Without warning, the captain entered the room. "Quiet, quiet, everyone!" he called out in a barely audible voice.

When the noise barely diminished, Billings looked over at Frank and cocked his head.

Frank cupped his hands around his mouth. "Sit down and shut up!" he bellowed in a deep, thunderous voice.

The hush was immediate.

The detective surveyed the room. The jail cell toward the back had a lone, drunk occupant, holding onto the bars and swaying from side to side. A uniformed policeman was banging down the receiver on a wall phone, and the Venetian blinds to Billing's office were shut tight.

"Look, the captain is gonna fill you guys in with what he has learned," Frank said. He turned to Billings. "Captain?"

Billings shifted over to the front of the room and loudly cleared his throat. He was clenching a newspaper in his fist. Crumpled slightly, the paper's headline, "Another Desmond Taylor Murder?" still loomed large enough to read at a distance.

"Okay, men. This is what we've got so far," he started. "A Medford Studios' producer, Chester Harris, was killed on January 4, at approximately 1:20 p.m. A clean rifle shot to the head. Forensics promises to tell us more by tomorrow."

The room buzzed as the men started talking among themselves.

The captain cleared his throat again and held up a hand. "Listen, listen. The Hearst outfit has already prepared a short *Metrotone News* film, which they've sent over for us to watch before they release it. Knowing Hearst and his muckraking ways, that isn't good for us. If they're already on top of this, we've gotta get out our own facts. And soon." He paused. "The higher ups at Medford have expressed to me directly how they don't want a panic on their hands, like when the director Desmond Taylor was killed back in '22, with no leads. They told me they'd do anything to stop that. I think you know what that means."

Several heads nodded, but Frank shook his. So, all this time, it was probably true. The captain was probably as crooked as the newly appointed, "Two Gun" Chief of Police James E. Davis, already toting his goon squad. Their motto? Get any suspect, no matter how, no matter who, and in the process, don't worry about money changing hands.

His eyes swept the room, sliding by some of the less guilty faces, resting on others who he knew were openly taking hefty bribes from the studio heads and the corrupt City Hall Gang.

Off to one side, an odd-looking middle-aged woman was none too politely being escorted outside, her shrill voice penetrating the room behind her.

He watched Billings shake his head at the woman, then motion with his index finger to a policeman standing against the northwest wall. The officer nodded, pulled down a screen attached to the ceiling by a series of rings, then dragged in a projector on a cart. Lights were switched off and a film started to roll.

Except for the movie projector clicking at a regular beat, the room grew silent as *Hearst Metrotone News* showed a Chester Harris image followed by a writer's card, explaining who he was. That was followed by an image of Medford Studios' front gate, then another writer's card, which described how as the producer lay dying, he moaned, "I have sinned!" More images of movie stars came after that, then more cards, full of the depravity of the Hollywood elite.

Pressed against the back of his chair, Frank cupped his hands behind his head. *This ain't good.*

He returned to an upright position and glanced over at Billings. The chief officer was scowling.

As soon as the lights came on, Williams, a rookie cop from Seattle spoke up. "How do they get these images and co-called facts so fast?"

"They make them up, and if we don't get cracking and arrest someone soon, we're going to be the laughing stock of the city," Billings snarled and pointed to a pegboard on the wall to his right. "So, here's our board with notes and photographs. You all know your teams. Just go out and get me a suspect."

Williams raised his hand. "Sir?"

Billings grit his teeth. "Yeah?"

"I was wondering if you could tell us what each team is gonna do. That's what we did when we trained in Seattle."

Chuckles rippled throughout the room.

"Well, good for you, officer. We're in Los Angeles now. We do it our way."

When several of the men applauded, the rookie's face turned bright red. Frank's heart sank. *Same old, same old.*

Billings approached him. "In my office, Detective Lozano. Now."

Inside the captain's office, he waved Frank toward a seat then plunked himself down onto a leather and rivet-back chair behind a massive mahogany desk. Elbows firmly on the blotter mat, hands folded, Billings leaned forward.

"Now, detective, what've you got for me?" he asked.

"Sir?"

"You were on the scene, you and your men questioned plenty of people. You must have gotten something out of it. We're under the gun now, so cough it up."

Bypassing Henry Blake, Eddie Willis suddenly popped into Frank's mind. Blake would be dealt with, but for now—

"Actually, I was planning on questioning someone. I'll get on it tonight."

"Yeah? Who?"

"Just some Houdini nothing who does stuff on the set."

Billings sat back. "Houdini?"

"Houdini," Frank repeated. "He disappears in his act. This guy was late onto the set. And apparently, he had had words with the victim at some point. A coincidence, wouldn't you say?"

Billings smirked. "Well, go after him, detective. And get him to talk, if you get my drift."

"Yes sir, I do." Frank paused. "Captain, what about the two other headshot killings? I mean—"

"Forget about those lost causes, Lozano. Just concentrate on this one. We're dealing with a big-time producer now."

Frank rose. "And another thing…"

Billings started tapping his fingers on his desktop.

"Who was that old dame giving us hell?" Frank asked.

Billings tossed out a sigh. "That's Sheila Morgan, Chester Harris' stepsister. A complete looney bin. Don't need someone like her right now." Looking down at the newspaper he had held up before, he waved Frank off.

Out on the street, Frank slid into his car to perform his engine startup routine. He didn't get far. Pulling out a flask, he took several fast shots, leaned his head back against the seat, and closed his eyes. A sudden image of Rosie's arm through Eddie's cropped up. *Christ.*

Mabel Sherman's Craftsman-style rooming house was shrouded in greenery. Nestled between two Spanish bungalows covered in bougainvillea, honeysuckle, and rosemary bushes, her spacious Hollywood home was her pride and joy. Wrapped around the house was a wide veranda, lending fine shade in the summer and a comfortable conversation spot for boarders each evening as the sun slowly drifted down toward the horizon.

The residence had served visitors for three decades. It had housed several migrant workers needing a temporary shelter before working in the fields as well as Loyola Marymount and California Institute of Technology students requiring a quiet ambiance for studying. More recently, it was sometimes home to young, fledgling actors, hoping to find fame and fortune in the movie industry. Following her parents' guidelines, Mabel demanded her three house rules be obeyed. First off, no unannounced guests. Second, no loud disturbances, and finally, total respect for all tenants abiding there.

Disliking late night callers, Mabel was clearly rankled when Frank rapped on her door at a little past ten o'clock and identified himself.

"How dare you come this time of night, Officer Lozano?"

"It's Detective Lozano, and I'm here on official police business." He stepped forward a pace. "What is your full name, ma'am?"

"Mabel Sherman's the name. Think of Mabel Normand and General Sherman. That oughta get you to remember me."

Frank snickered. "I doubt if I'll ever forget you, Mabel."

She drew herself up. "Mrs. Sherman, you mean."

His sigh let out a blast of gin. "As I said, I'm here to talk to Eddie Willis."

"What for? He's a grand fellow. He helps me all the time around here. Everyone loves him."

"Police business, Mrs. Sherman. Now, will you take me to him, or do I have to come in using force?"

For a couple of seconds, she squinted her eyes in assessment. Then she shrugged, showed him in, and led him down a long hallway toward the back of the house.

As he walked, he noticed quite a few photographs graced the walls. Most were headshots, some were signed, but most not. Mixed in were pictures of Los Angeles. When he passed a wall telephone, he stopped, backtracked to it, and jotted down the number before moving on.

Mabel was already in front of a room labeled No. 5, tapping her right foot. When he approached, she knocked gently on the door.

No answer.

He nodded, and she tried again, just as softly.

"Stand aside." He moved to the door and pounded on it.

He could hear some shuffling on the other side of the door. Soon he heard a deadbolt being unlatched, and the door opened. Eddie stood in the doorway, in a bathrobe and pajamas, his brown hair tousled, his blue eyes blinking.

"So sorry to wake you, hon." Mabel moved in front of Frank and flipped her thumb back toward the detective. "This here policeman says he wants to talk to you."

"Remember me, Eddie?"

Eddie stared for a moment. Then, "Sure. What's this about, detective?"

The detective pushed past Eddie into the small room, ignoring Mabel's "How *dare* you!"

"Close the door, Willis," Frank said. "We need to talk."

Eddie closed the door and sat on the bed. "Okay. What do you want from me?"

"You had a problem with Harris. I need to know more about that. You mentioned you worked things out and got help from Lon Chaney, right? By the way, tell me again, what is it you do exactly?"

Eddie sighed. "A little bit of everything, like carpentry, makeup for Mr. Chaney, run errands."

"Hmm. I heard different." Frank had a sudden itch to lean on Eddie even further.

"Just what and who did you hear this from?" Eddie asked. "Pete Roberts? Look, detective, he's got a thing for Rosie. He'll say anything to get me in trouble."

"We'll see about that," Frank muttered.

"Say, I thought they usually interrogated people down at the police station, not ten o'clock at night in their bedrooms."

Frank could feel his blood begin to boil. He sank down on the room's only chair and stared at Eddie. "We're doin' it my way tonight, okay?" He surveyed the room and then stood up.

Eddie shrugged and turned to see what Frank saw.

"What the hell is in there?" Frank asked. He walked over to a standing cabinet, opened it up, and took out a rifle. "Hello. What've we got here?"

Eddie visibly paled. "That's a gift from my uncle who was killed in the war. My aunt gave it to me."

Frank turned the rifle over. "It's got a scope and everything."

"Be careful. I'm trying to keep it in mint condition. But you can check it out, detective. It's not been fired for a long time. Smell it, if you don't believe me."

Lozano sniffed it. *Damn. Definitely hasn't been fired recently.* Reluctantly, he put it back and shut the cabinet door, Billings' last words of "get him to talk" rattling around in his brain.

"We still will want to see you at the station, Willis. I'll let you know when."

He walked to the door and turned the doorknob. Suddenly, he swung around. "How deep is your connection to Miss Paige?"

"What?" Eddie's eyes widened. He strode over to the door and yanked it open with a bang. "If you're done, detective, I have an early call tomorrow morning."

It was as if the car had a mind of its own. Before he knew it, Frank was stationed across the street and down a ways from the Highland Courts. He put his car in idle. With his lights off and from his angle, he could see her sitting out on the Paige apartment steps talking with an older man.

Why did he feel such a pull toward her? God only knew. It had been so long since he'd let anyone in. But why this girl?

He shook his head and took out his flask. He guzzled three more swigs and swept the back-of-his hand over his mouth. Then he gave a sudden chuckle.

Rosie stood up, and for several seconds gyrated like some hoochie-coochie girl. Then she plopped down almost like a rag doll. What were they were talking about? He let the clutch out. Slowly, carefully, he drove down the street. Once past the Courts, he switched on the lights and gathered speed.

By the time he trudged up the steps of his modest apartment, he could hear his wall clock inside chiming twelve times. Midnight. He fumbled with the lock. Then, staggering inside, he instantly knocked over a chair, which sent him flying onto his sofa.

He stayed there for several minutes, inert, crumpled up in an odd, twisted position. Torn window shades were yellowed in wear and tear. Numerous empty gin bottles lay about, wrinkled clothes lay strewn across the room in a hazardous pattern, and a large pile of dirty, food encrusted dishes were stacked up in his kitchen sink. Finally, he raised his head to concentrate on a nearby framed photograph of him and two children. *They ain't even gonna remember me* was his last thought before he passed out.

December 21, 1925
Two Weeks BEFORE the Harris Shooting
7 p.m.

In the darkest corner of the already dimly lit Peachtree restaurant, Chester Harris sat amongst his gambling cronies and held court. Glasses of soda water and backstairs gin hovered around plates of leftover steak and potato tidbits, as their intense discussion turned even blacker than the physical surroundings.

"I don't give a hoot about how they do business," Harris said, his voice lowered to a growl. "I'm not going to pay up immediately, just because they say so."

One of his colleagues raked his fingers through his hair. "Look, Chester, when you're dealing with both the Ardizzone mob and the City Hall Gang, you just cough it up. Period," he said in a pinched voice.

Chester Harris' lips curled into a sneer. "I'm not some hayseed, you know. I run a good movie set, and I know how to grease things up with the big fellas. One good day at the dog track, and I'm good to go. They don't scare me. Remember, I deal with the movie moguls all the time, and they're tough as nails. Why, at one point, I was friendly with Adolph Zuckor, head of the Famous Players-Lasky studio, and they used to call him 'Creepy.'"

"You got no idea who you're dealing with, Harris," another man piped up.

Abruptly, Chester stood up and flung a ten-dollar bill on the table. "For my meal, and then some." He headed off toward a side exit. Like many times before, he didn't feel like running into any studio folk coming in from the front entrance.

That was a big mistake. Five feet shy of the side door, he was yanked over to a checkerboard cloth-covered table so hard, a glass fell over. The freshly made gin fizz instantly seeped out like an oozing wound.

"Come with me, Harris," a thick-necked man with an Italian accent snarled. His huge belly, cinched tight with a thin belt, made him look all the more ridiculous.

Without thinking, Harris snorted. Another mistake.

"Where you going, Harris, huh? Not without paying up first," the big Belly said with a loud belch.

Harris drew himself up. "Tell your bosses I'll deal with my debts the way I want. They'll get their money, all right."

"When?" A second man asked.

"When I say so."

"Suit yourself," the pudgy man said, smirking.

Outside, the air held a slight chill—the kind of night that had once been perfect for cuddling up with Henry Blake after ferociously passionate sex. If he closed his eyes, he could picture how fulfilled and relieved he had felt to find something outside of the marriage with his shrewish wife. Did he make a blunder by ditching Henry? Naw, the sniveling little guy was getting tiresome, and besides—

Slammed up against a wall, Harris faced an unfamiliar man. A beefy-looking chowder head had his giant paw wrapped around the producer's neck and squeezed it so hard, Harris gasped for breath. Beyond the roughneck stood the City Hall dandy, Kane Kent Parrot, along with his partner, the sophisticated Charles H. Crawford. Both men's faces were etched in scowls.

"Ready to listen, Mr. Rich Guy, Mr. Swell?" Parrot asked calmly.

Harris made an odd choking sound.

"Let him go," Parrot muttered to their henchman. The goon released his hold.

Crawford spoke next. "I don't think you realize the position you're in, Harris. It's really quite simple. When we say pay up, you pay up. And don't even think about getting any outside help. Number one, you're as dirty as they come—in more ways than one, I might add—and two, we happen to know some top people in this town."

"Get it?" Parrot asked. "This is your last warning. The money is in our hands by Thursday. Or else."

January 1, 1926
Three Days BEFORE the Harris Shooting
8:50 p.m.

Henry Blake's hand shook as he picked up the receiver and tried to sound normal. "Hello?" he said. He listened for several seconds, took a large gulp, and answered. "I know, I know. How much money would something like that cost?" His words sounded strange to him, as if he were in a foreign country, trying hard to sound proficient in a language he really didn't understand.

He gulped again, his Adam's apple flipping up and down. "When and where do I pay him?" A few more seconds of listening gave him his answer. He nodded, then realized he needed to actually say something. "All right. I can meet him there at that time. I just want Chester Harris finished."

CHAPTER FOUR

*"I'm a curiosity in Hollywood.
I'm a big freak, because I'm myself."*
— Clara Bow, the "It Girl" actress

January 7, 1926
Three Days AFTER the Harris Shooting

OFF IN A corner of *The Runaway* set, Rosie glanced down the row of female extras sitting next to her. A bevy of brown crimped hair, golden ringlets, and wavy brunette locks met her gaze. Chatting, giggling, the young girls only silenced when they leaned in toward their individual mirrors to apply a thick smear of blue-toned greasepaint on their faces and an odd-hued yellow for their lips.

Because of the cameras' film sensitivities, how actors' faces appeared was crucial. So, Medford, in its infinite wisdom, had provided each actor and actress with a special "How to Apply Your Makeup" manual. But Rosie learned as soon as she joined ranks there, she had a problem. When she had first come to Los Angeles, she worked for RKO, and their instructions were the polar opposite of Medford's. She still remembered trying to keep up with the Medford players when she first arrived, and how she had to keep studying the open book before her in order to get it right.

"At RKO, we applied the greasepaint after the yellow lip paint, not like it says here," she murmured several times during her first few days at the new studio.

The girl next to her had laughed. "Welcome to Medford, honey."

Now, seasoned at Medford and outfitted in a simple frock, thick stockings, and clunky shoes, Rosie smiled. *What an important set today. Clara Bow. My goodness!*

Suddenly, she realized the other girls were much farther along in their makeup process than she was. Her right hand moved like lightning as she smeared the greasy yellow substance onto her lips and the bluish tone grease on her face.

Next came the hand-thickened dark eyebrows—which didn't really match her auburn hair— and enough mascara to make a raccoon envious.

With the background sound of chairs scraping on wood, she took one last scan in the mirror and performed a clown smile to test for cracks in the makeup around her eyes. Satisfied she looked halfway decent, she hurried along behind the others, just in time to get a full megaphone blast from the director, Bert Weston.

"Get on the set. Time is money!" he bellowed. People scrambled to line up in front of him.

She noticed a young child had quietly joined them, and in spite of the barking tyrant, she winked at the boy. The blond, blue-eyed dewdrop of a child sidestepped closer to her. She looked down at him, assessing he was probably no older than five years old. Rosie sensed his nervousness when he clutched at her hand. She enclosed it fully as Weston continued shouting about his full inspection coming up before they could begin shooting.

A heavy-set man with an ascot slightly skewed and a jacket too tight, the director's Napoleonic reputation was legendary. As he lectured, Rosie noticed a large food stain on his shirt and a button undone over his extended belly. *How disgusting he is.* She looked around the set for Eddie, who had mentioned he was looking forward to being on the same set as her today.

She spied him across the room, hammering a last-minute nail posthaste into a wooden structure. After a single whack, he turned and gave her their secret signal to meet up later at some point—a scratch of his head and a tiny finger salute at his brow.

She smiled. Then frowned as Weston made his way over to their group. *What a tyrant.* As he strolled through the line of extras and scrutinized each actor's appearance, she heard him sputter lots of comments.

"All right. Could be better...*not* acceptable," he muttered through the ranks, until he got to Rosie. And the boy.

He shook his head vehemently. "No, no, no. Both your eyes! Girlie, your green eyes just won't work," he growled. "Make sure to stay in the background today. Only crowd scenes for you!"

"I beg your pardon?" Rosie asked. She fought an urge to slap him.

He ignored her. "And as for you, kid, your blue eyes is gonna ruin me. Don't have time to replace you. Damn!" He shook his head. "Wolf eyes. Scary. Norma Shearer had that blue eye problem, and D.W. Griffith called her out on it. Told her she'd never go far."

Thanks for the history lesson. Rosie drew a deep breath. She put her arm around the boy, whose cheeks were slick with tears.

"You're fine just as you are," she said softly. "Don't pay him no mind. He's crazy."

While the cameras were placed on their tripods and the painted scenery dropped behind them, the boy squeezed her hand twice.

"There, there," she murmured and leaned over to kiss him on the top of his head. His upward look of appreciation was enough to mentally shelve Weston into his proper place. She grinned.

But their mutual moment of peace was quickly shattered.

"Girlie, boy, times a wasting! Go get into your proper places. You, girl, go off to the side, behind the others. You, boy, go to the marker like I told you." Weston's bullhorn was blasting only inches away.

Jarred, they both scattered, the boy to a little drawn "X" on front stage, Rosie to the far back of the crowd on stage right.

This oughta do it. Can't yell at me anymore.

She was wrong. "Hey girlie, duck down!" he bellowed.

"What?" she snapped.

"You heard me. I told you, you can't even be seen!"

The several breath-intakes coming from the cast were heartening. At least other people recognized his ruthlessness. She glanced over at Eddie. His jaw was set, and she could only imagine how tightly clenched his fists were.

She scrunched down further. "Is this hidden enough, Mr. Weston?" she called out, peeking out through the crook of a large man's bent elbow.

He whipped around, his eyes flashing.

She steeled herself for another outburst from him, but it never came.

"Well, hello, Miss Bow," he said. "I didn't see you standing over there.

Welcome to my set." Weston's voice was unrecognizable, it was so warm and welcoming.

The entire cast ensemble applauded. Off to the side, Rosie stepped out from the crowd and clapped hard. She glanced down. Her palms had turned pink.

Meanwhile, Weston had put his arm through Clara Bow's and led the celebrity over to front stage center next to the boy to begin the scene. The celebrity gave the go-ahead nod, and the cameraman started rolling his camera at top speed.

She held up her hand. "Wait a minute, wait a minute. Mr. Weston?"

Rosie watched his startled eyes widen then retract.

"Yes, Miss Bow? What's the problem?" He actually sounded nervous.

Rosie stifled a laugh.

"Why are the cameras going so fast?"

He sighed. "That's my new technique. The faster the reel, the less time it takes. Time is money, Miss Bow. I guarantee you, the studio heads will love it."

Stock-still, she shook her head. "I actually like quality, Mr. Weston, don't you? Could we please try it at regular speed, just for me?" She batted her eyes twice.

He gulped. "All right. Let's do it again. For you." He sounded slightly less cordial.

"I'm assuming I won't get shot with a rifle, will I?" She grinned.

Rosie's loud pig snort resonated from the right side of the set.

"At least there's one person here who gets my humor." Clara turned toward the stage right crowd.

Weston didn't utter a word, but when he picked up his megaphone again, he followed Clara's gaze for a second before continuing on.

"Here we go. Ready? ACTION!" he barked.

Peeking out from behind the large actor, Rosie followed every move the actress made. Mesmerized, she noticed how Clara turned this way and that, her lovely eyes, mouth, and face always expressive, her small nuanced hand movements, riveting.

Rosie stepped out a little further. Now that's someone to aspire to. *Look how she can go from comedy to drama in a flash.*

Weston megaphoned, "Cut!"

Clara instantly smiled and turned to the cast and crew. "Good job, everyone."

"Yes, good job, everyone," Weston repeated.

A smirk suddenly appeared on Clara's face. She turned to Weston. "You must be so proud of your ensemble here, Mr. Weston. A truly outstanding group, and I'm sure you're dying to tell them all that."

"Yes, yes." Beads of perspiration coated his brow.

Rosie grinned smugly. *Clara Bow is marvelous. Can't wait to tell Mama and Walt about this.*

She looked over at Eddie, who looked highly amused.

Just then one of the bit players tiptoed over to Clara with a headshot photo and pen in hand.

Clara nodded and scribbled something on the picture. When the girl turned to go, the celebrity patted her on the shoulder.

"No fraternizing with the stars!" Weston hollered.

The star turned to say something, but just then the little boy also approached her. Smiling tenderly, she wrote something down on his slip of paper and gave him a quick hug. He smiled broadly and happily jogged back to his station as Clara strolled over to a little side dressing table to reapply her makeup.

Weston viewed the exchange without a word.

As the child trotted by the director, everyone watched in horror as Weston stuck his leg out.

The boy went flying.

"Hey, *hey!* That's not all right!" Eddie shouted out in a deep voice. He tore over to the boy and knelt down. "Are you all right, son?" He stroked the boy's hair.

The child nodded slowly, his eyes still looking dazed.

Weston charged over, his teeth clenched. "You're outta here, Willis. And don't come back!"

Even with Clara present, Weston had lost his cool. Rosie watched Eddie give the boy one last head pat. Then he marched over to his working area where he shoved his hammer into his tool kit, and without even a backward glance at her, charged out, his boots scuffing loudly on the wooden floor.

When murmurs and light applause took over the room at Eddie's exit, Weston whipped around and scanned the room carefully. Then, he lifted his megaphone. "Time for the next scene," he barked.

Clara returned, and without even a glance in his direction, took her position and waited, one hand on her hip, the other patting her hair.

By two o'clock another break was announced. Weston, obviously past caring about the celebrity's presence, fast-paced it to the exit. On his way out, a slight ripple of chuckles cropped up as Clara turned toward the actors. Rosie was performing a mock salute to Weston's back.

Clara giggled. "Well, I'll be," she said.

As soon as he left, the famous actress tossed back her head and roared.

"Well, folks," she called out, "let's get in some rest and relaxation. That's sure *not* gonna happen when you-know-who returns."

The room erupted in laughter.

Rosie wandered over to get some water from one of the pitchers lined up on a side cloth-covered table. *Where did Eddie go? Did he leave the lot or is he waiting for me at our spot?*

Pete Roberts came over. "So, I see Eddie's not here. Again. Just like the day of the shooting. Interesting, don't you think?"

Rosie stared at him. "I don't know what you mean."

He returned her stare. "I think you do, Rosie. In fact, I bet you've been wondering about it yourself."

When she whipped around to return to her stage right crowd, she ran headlong into Clara.

"Miss Bow, so sorry!" she exclaimed.

"Nonsense. No harm done." Clara leaned in close. "What's your name?"

"Rose—Rosie Paige."

"Well, Rose—Rosie Paige, you've got gumption! I like people with gumption."

They grinned at each other.

Clara took a step back, her head cocked. "You got a fella, honey?"

"Why, yes. The guy who got kicked off the set, as a matter of fact."

"What? The he-man with a heart? Zowie! Now he's a catch!"

Red-faced, Rosie nodded. "Yes, I suppose so. Now, if only my mama would agree, the world would be a perfect place."

"Oh?" Clara's cherubic mouth had formed a perfect "O."

Rosie sighed. "According to my mama, he's not good enough for me." *I can't believe I'm telling her all this.*

"Oh, honey. I sure know about that one. Mamas can be a drain on the system. I know my own one was, that's for damn sure."

"I don't get it. He's been nothing but nice and polite to her, but she keeps saying he's not a rich producer or director. Says he'll never amount to anything. Be broke all his life, that kind of thing. But I know there's more to it."

"And your father? What's he say?"

Rosie shrugged and looked past the actress. "He left us years ago."

"Ah-hah. That explains a lot." Clara seemed lost in thought. Finally, she drew a deep breath. "None of us have a crystal ball, do we? Who knows in the movie biz. Tomorrow your fella could be head producer or director!" She laughed. "He'd probably do a better job than Weston, that's for damn sure."

Both chuckled, followed by several seconds of silence.

"Is he good in the bed department?" Clara asked.

Rosie looked down, her face crimson-red.

"Oh, my goodness. You haven't done it yet? My, oh my, you are an old-fashioned girl, aren't you? Better not tell the other actresses. They'll have a field day!"

She looked both ways, then, turning around and lifting up her skirt, she pulled out a very small silver flask from underneath her right garter. Immediately, she grabbed a quick swig. It was when she started to put it back that she paused. Handing it over to Rosie she said, "My gift to you. Here's to losing your virginity at the right time and with the right man. Enjoy, honey. Stow it under your dress."

Rosie held the little flask and looked up. "For me? Why?"

"Because I like you. In fact, why don't you come to a party I'm giving this Saturday night?"

"Really?"

"Of course. Now, you ain't gonna see the usual Hollywood celebrities there. I don't get invited to those hotsy-totsy shindigs, so I just started giving my own get-togethers."

"That's fine with me. Can I bring Eddie?"

"You sure can! We can always use a handsome fella around!"

Weston wandered back into the room, his face beet-red, his eyes blinking.

"Look at the drunk who just walked in. He looks positively ossified! Maybe Eddie should replace him," Clara whispered, shaking her head. "Quick, hide the flask!"

Rosie shoved it down into her brassiere and hunched over.

"Places, people, places," he blasted into the megaphone.

"Ah, Miss Bow?" Rosie asked.

"Clara, it's Clara."

"All right then, Clara. What should we wear?"

"Just some pretty dress. Nothing fancy. And as for your fella, nothing elegant. We ain't the H.E."

Weston glowered at the two of them. "That means you, girlie!" he barked at Rosie.

"H.E.?" Rosie mouthed.

Clara reached out and grabbed her arm. "H.E.—Hollywood Elite," she said as they both took their places.

The scene went well, the camera was taken down, and Rosie kept thinking of Eddie. *Must check our secret place before going home. After all, Clara definitely approves of him!*

She was gathering up her makeup kit when one of the extras snuggled up close to her.

"I saw you taking a tiny nip with Miss Bow," she whispered. "You're not such a babe-in-the woods, after all, are you?"

"I beg your pardon?"

"Yeah, you should beg my pardon." The girl laughed. "The name's Gertie, and I thought you might like to learn how to secure that little piece of hardware you got under your dress."

Rosie's eyes grew round.

"Forget about behind the front of your dress. I'll show you how to tie it around your garter belt. If you don't, one quick move and bam! It's hittin' the floor and it's goodbye, Rosie!"

"How do you know my name?"

"I got ears, don't I?" Gertie laughed and patted Rosie's shoulder. "I overheard you and Miss Bow, is all. She sure is the cat's meow, ain't she? It's just so unfair the way the press treats her sometimes. Anyway, come with me to the ladies' bathroom, and I'll show you how I secure mine. And as payment, you can give me a swallow or two."

Giggling, the actress wove her arm through Rosie's and steered them both toward the exit. Just shy of the door, Rosie stopped.

"Wait, I want to wave goodbye to Clara."

Gertie laughed. "Be my guest, but I think she's already gone."

When Rosie looked around, she observed the star had indeed left. But Pete Roberts hadn't. He was across the room by his camera, staring at her.

CHAPTER FIVE

"A closed mind is a dying mind."
— Edna Ferber, author

**January 8, 1926
Four Days AFTER the Harris Shooting**

THE LATE AFTERNOON'S light sliced through the Venetian blinds in the Paige kitchen. While Rosie and Walt sat in the cozy, wood-planked breakfast nook, a large steak sizzled in a frying pan on the range, lending a tantalizing smell everywhere. Potatoes browned in another, smaller pan, and two pieces of toast popped up from the brand-new Heat Master toaster.

Rosie sighed and took a large sip from her water glass. "Really, Walt? Giving me such an earful so late in the day?"

"Walt's just looking after you, dear," Beatrice said as she opened up the oak icebox, took out a butter dish, and placed it on the red checker cloth-covered table. Next, three hearty dinners were doled out onto well-worn plates. With her new, starched apron on, her movements were fast and experienced. But Rosie noticed something else. Her mother's lips were tightly pursed.

Oh, boy. Here comes another round of disapproval.

"All we're saying is Clara Bow's got a bad reputation," her mother said. "She's been known to have sex with lots of men. And that's not you, dear.

You're a decent girl." She lay the loaded plates down on the table and squeezed in next to her daughter. "Not like that harlot. Not like a lot of the other actresses who come into the fitting room. I could tell you things…" Beatrice paused, as if she were about to say more. Instead, she sat in silence.

Across from them, Walt nodded as he shoveled down food. After several swallows of ice tea, he leaned back and patted his stomach. "Yeah, I've heard that, too. A real floozy. Not like you, Rosie-Posey." He produced a weak smile.

Rosie wasn't buying. "Well, she was truly nice on the set. And not just to me. To everyone else, too." As she took another sip, she caught Walt and her mother exchange glances. "She was a lot nicer than that director, I can tell you that! Nicer than that Chester Harris, who—" She paused and gulped. "Sorry. I know it's not nice to talk ill about the dead."

"Yeah, I heard Harris wasn't so nice. Well, I suppose he got his." Walt picked up the morning's newspaper and turned back to its front page.

"Any more news about the killer, Walt?" Beatrice asked.

When he slowly shook his head, she dropped another piece of bread in the toaster for him.

Rosie turned to Walt. "I'm curious. Where did you get that information about Clara?"

"Ah, Clara now, is it?" he said. "Hearst's *Los Angeles Examiner*, if you must know."

"Eddie says Hearst makes up things, just to sell newspapers," Rosie said. "And by the way, Clara invited Eddie, too, so I will be fully chaperoned."

"Eddie." Beatrice snorted. "What does he know? That hayseed!"

Rosie fixed her hands on her hips. "I don't get it. What do you have against Eddie? Mama, you told me you didn't like me taking the Red Trolley car all the time, so now Eddie's been driving me around in his own car. By the way, he's a real safe driver. Knows all about cars, too. We go to the movies, to parks, up to Mulholland Drive near the Hollywoodland sign, all over the place, really. But I've already told you that. You're always complaining about him, but at least he's been steady. Not like the two other boys I dated when we were here that first year. You know how hurt I was when each one dropped me like a hot potato. Doesn't do much for a girl's confidence, much less her heart."

Beatrice huffed. "Well, they were fools. I just don't want you to end up like I did, Rosie. You don't need a no-account husband who'll end up leaving you flat broke with a baby. A husband who wore fancy clothes an' all, strutting around like a peacock, but in the end, was a lousy salesman and spent all our money so I was forced to go out and sew my fingers to the bone for customers, while he took off days on end, God knows where. A husband who—" She looked over at Rosie who was staring at her mother. "Well," Beatrice said, straightening up. "That's all in the past."

"Is it, Mama?" Rosie asked softly. She remembered her mother's terse admission regarding Eddie after the two of them had first met.

For several seconds the wall clock's ticks took over the room.

Beatrice's brow furrowed. "Seems to me you and Eddie have gotten too cozy. You two go off every Saturday."

"Yes, we do. What's the big deal?"

"The big deal is he's got no ambition. Isn't that so, Walt?" Beatrice turned to him.

Walt shrugged. "I suppose not."

"Walt, you'll agree with anything Mama says," Rosie muttered.

"Rosie! Have more respect for Walt. We owe him that much. Besides, he knows his way around Hollywood. Why, he was there on Staten Island, New York, very early on, helping on the set of *Perils of Pauline*. Walt, isn't that so?"

He grunted.

"He knows who's gonna make it and who isn't," Beatrice said. "Isn't that right, Walt?"

He looked over at Rosie. "All's I was thinking was that instead of going off with Eddie all the time, you and your mother could see my Hollywood collection sometime. There are things I've gotten over the years and during my time in the film world."

Rosie pointed to the black No. 3 Brownie camera on the table in front of him. "Is that why you're always taking pictures? And by the way, what exactly did you do in the early years of movie making, Walt? Did you also work out here? Mama's never told me anything about your background."

"Yes, I did work a little out here. I did a little bit of everything—carpentry, helping camera men set up, that kind of thing."

"You see, Mama?" Rosie smiled. "Walt and Eddie have a lot in common." She turned to Walt. "Why did you stop working in the film business?"

"Truth is, Rosie, I just got tired of it, is all. Tired of the stars and movie moguls getting richer and richer, while the rest of us Joes had to work long hours with little pay."

An awkward silence followed as Beatrice cleared the dishes and put them in soapy water in the freestanding sink. Walt turned back to his paper. And after a few minutes, Beatrice sat down again, took a sip of her coffee, and snickered.

"Behind the scenes, these movie stars aren't so great, you know," she said.

Rose raised one eyebrow.

"I can tell you what they're talking about in the studio's costume room about America's little sweetheart, Mary Pickford." Beatrice paused dramatically then leaned in toward the table. "I heard the other day that Miss Pickford's lovely curls aren't all her own." She put a hand over her mouth and giggled.

"Oh?" Rosie asked.

"Yeah. They say she does has some of her own, of course, but that she also supplements her locks with other people's."

"Yeah, so?" Rosie grinned. She was grateful for the mood and topic change.

A mischievous look inched across her mother's face. "She supplements her curls with local hair."

"That's not so unusual, Mama," Rosie said. *Where's this going?*

Beatrice grinned. "Yeah, but her local sources are hookers."

All their cackles felt good. *Thank God.* Then, after the three of them proceeded to swap more anecdotes about the behind-the-scenes-tough-as-nails movie star, Walt took a couple of photos of the two women and went home. Rosie said goodnight and retreated to her bedroom while Beatrice was left in the living room, to pore over her movie magazines.

Safe in her own little haven, Rosie lay down on the bed, her eyes closing the second she felt the softness of the down comforter against her back. The room had been her sanctuary ever since they had arrived in Los Angeles. Plump, homemade pillows—courtesy of her mama—were strategically placed on the bed and on an armchair. Books on nature, art, and animals were stacked next to classic and bestselling novels on her bowed bookcase. No evidence of movie magazines. She had made it clear that was her mother's domain. She also had insisted on keeping a framed family photograph with her wedged in between her parents, taken just before her father had deserted them. For the past two years, it had remained on her bedside table. During her first year in Los Angeles, she noticed how Beatrice cringed slightly each time she passed the photo to kiss her girl goodnight. Still, Rosie refused to toss it out. These days she was relieved that it was no longer an issue. Obviously, her mother had finally accepted its importance to Rosie.

Lying on the bed now, she drew a deep breath and let her mind drift. *Eddie.* Why hadn't he met up with her at their special spot after the Weston outburst? Would Lon Chaney back him up this time? If not, would he be able to get more jobs at Medford, so they could see each other during the day? Or would he have to go elsewhere, separating them? She pictured how they first met at Medford Studios. How he had not only touched her emotionally, but also, to her surprise, his handsome masculinity had awakened certain physical yearnings.

She could feel the sting of tears forming. *Oh, Eddie, why'd you have to be such a hero?* Then she felt ashamed. Wasn't helping that boy one of the reasons why she was attracted to him? He was always standing up for people—in his rooming house and even vagabonds on the street.

She covered her eyes and sighed. Then why did she sometimes get so conflicted around him? One moment, she felt comforted and secure, the next, a feeling of bad things to come would overcome her. She let her mind drift further back.

"Never trust them, Rosie, no matter how considerate or loving they may seem. It's just not worth it," was her mama's motto that, over the years, had embedded itself into Rosie's psyche. By the time they had arrived in Los Angeles, the young girl had automatically developed a thick, self-protective skin.

But working at RKO and Medford Studios, she soon ran into trouble. Being a "good girl" made her feel like a fish out of water amongst the wide breadth of questionable morals most of the studio girls had often chatted about. Rosie would spend long days listening to their stories, then go home to her mother's tight reins and subtle warnings from their new friend and advisor, Walt.

Lying under the covers, she suddenly thought of Mark Oliver. How friendly and nice he had seemed, standing in line next to her at a local grocery market. Their easy banter and common love for animals was the perfect escape for her at the time. New to Los Angeles, she had established little contacts other than her mother and Walt.

During their two months together, Mark introduced her to her veterinarian, Dr. Peterson, and showed her Santa Monica beach, where she delighted in its clean air and soft waves. Attracted to him physically, he was her first foray into a romantic relationship, despite Beatrice's watchful eye. Naïve in these matters, she was surprised she wanted to taste more.

But he suddenly stopped calling. A fluke? Or was her mama right about all men?

Willy Sweet popped up next in her mind. An errand boy for RKO Studios, she had met him on the trolley. Handsome in a rugged way, she learned he was also gentle at heart. And so funny. For four months, they would sometimes sit on a park bench together at the end of their separate workdays, where he would regale her with one hilarious movie rumor after another. In between her bursts of laughter, she could tell she was falling for him. And then came her first real kiss. It was a gate-opener. Although Beatrice told her she wasn't impressed by his credentials, Rosie felt he might be the one for her.

But it happened again. Willy stopped calling as well, and soon a fine film of doubt worked its way into her ego. *What am I doing wrong? Mama can't be right, can she?* She even thought of going over to RKO to see him, but at the last moment, a tiny seed of self-pride stopped her.

Safe on her bed, thinking back on all of this now, she turned somber. After Willy came Eddie on one of the Medford sets. To her surprise, he had stayed steady ever since, despite his first meeting with Beatrice.

That sure was a disaster from beginning to end. Bottom line? Beatrice told her that Eddie reminded her too much of Johnny Paige, her no-good, cheating husband. End of discussion.

Abruptly, Rosie could feel her heartbeat race, even now on her bed. *Did all men have this lasting effect when they leave? Would that be her fate with Eddie someday?*

January 2, 1926
Two Nights BEFORE the Harris Shooting

Henry Blake figured the site the person on the phone had picked would probably be a good spot for the payoff. Close enough to Medford's front entrance to have no confusion as to its locale, yet covert and dark from the lack of street lamps. That fact had served him well for clandestine meet ups with certain men in his life, although of course, Chester Harris, being above the average Joe, the *hoi polloi*, so to speak, would never agree to that. He'd made sure the two of them either rendezvoused at Henry's own villa or, on the rare occasion, a hasty trip up to Julian Eltinge's separate hideout—a tiny cabin on the northeast end of his property.

As Henry stood back in the shadowy darkness, he could hear hurried footsteps coming down the block toward him. His heart pumping, he self-consciously fingered the overly stuffed envelope as little gasps of air eked out of his throat. *Just get this over with.* The footsteps appeared almost on top of him.

"You, Henry Blake?" a deep voice asked.

The man's face wasn't clear, but his cocked fedora and lit cigar were front and center.

"Yes, I am." Henry's concerted effort to sound tough fell flat. His voice ended in a tiny squeak.

"So, you got what I came for?" The man's impatience was clear.

Henry started to hand over the envelope, but at the last moment, held onto it for dear life. A slight tug of war came next, until the man muttered, "I'm getting paid to get this, so cough it up. Or else."

Henry let go. "This should take care of what was discussed, right? I'm giving all the information I was asked about. And the money."

The man grunted. "Yeah, yeah. All's good. You'll see."

To Henry's horror, someone walked by just at that moment. *Damn!* It was someone from the studio. *What is his name?* And then he remembered. The cameraman, Pete Roberts.

Henry tried to hide his face as the Fedora guy walked away, but he sensed Roberts slowed down his step deliberately because he recognized him.

As Henry proceeded down the block to his car, several thoughts permeated his mind: *Hope Roberts didn't recognize me. Hope my money will get to the right person,* and *Chester, God help me, if all goes well, you're going to reap what you sowed.*

CHAPTER SIX

*"There's no such thing as good money, or bad money.
There's just money."*
— Charlie "Lucky" Luciano, mobster

January 10, 1926
Six Days AFTER the Harris Shooting

FUNNY HOW DIFFERENT a set can be when the director is pleasant. Rosie stepped into her assigned area. Today it was the *Love 'em and Leave 'em* movie with Evelyn Brent and the actress people were really beginning to talk about—Louise Brooks. The director, Frank Tuttle, seemed very nice. *Okay, maybe he was simply normal.* Hearing someone behind her echo her feelings, she turned around and grinned. There was the flask-securing instructor herself, Gertie, who grinned back.

Dressed as flappers, Gertie, Rosie, and two others awaited instructions.

"Hope we get used today," Gertie said.

"What do you mean?" Rosie asked.

"They'll be shooting a love scene first, and if there's time, they'll do another scene with us. That's what I heard, anyway," Gertie commented.

Rosie said nothing. The thought of watching a real live love scene sped up her pulse.

"Hey, you still wearing that little flask under your garter belt?" Gertie whispered.

Rosie nodded, touching her dress self-consciously.

"When the shoot's over, let's have some hooch, okay?"

Distracted by Eddie's sudden appearance, she nodded slowly. "Sure," she muttered.

When he saw her, he smiled and made their private signal.

She smiled back but couldn't help thinking of her mama's frequent commentary. Was Eddie the real McCoy, or was he going to be like Mark and Willy and leave her?

Tuttle picked up his megaphone and turned to the bit players. "All right, ladies, please go off to the side of the bedroom set we'll be using today. Just wait in the wings."

Gertie snorted. "What did I tell you?"

Rosie and the girls were guided past a fabricated bedroom, with lush, floor-to-ceiling curtains, a satin bedcover, a dressing table, and what looked to be giant puppets placed strategically across an opulent chaise lounge.

Puppets? What kind of film is this?

She soon found out. Standing deep in the shadows, she watched Louise Brooks and the suave Lawrence Gray begin a love scene. Instantly, she could see why the actress was garnering so much public attention. That "bobbed" hair look was mesmerizing. Short, dark, and sleek, on her head it almost looked sculpted.

Sudden visions of the little china doll she had seen in an Omaha shop window so long ago cropped up. It had been a rare Saturday, one when her mother wasn't working. Eight years old, and the little girl was relentless. Over and over again, she had pestered her mother to buy it for her, but Beatrice had forever stood firm. Finally, after hours of this behavior, the abandoned woman snapped. "No!" she screamed. "We've been left penniless. I can't afford anything. You can thank your father for that!"

The steady crank of the camera rolling brought her back to reality. Concentrating on every movement, every nuance, she watched Louise Brooks, decked out in a shiny black dress, walk over to a dressing table and pick up a powder puff attached to a long stick. As the actor Gray stood nearby studying her the entire time, she coquettishly patted her face, then ambled over to the chaise lounge where she lay down, and hugged the two puppets to her chest.

Rosie marveled at how sophisticated the actor looked as he stood there casually holding his cigarette and leaning against a chair. How above it all he seemed. He could do anything he wanted, she figured. And he did. He put down his smoke and charged over to Louise. With a swift, hard movement, he tossed the puppets on the floor and sank down next to her.

As he leaned across the actress, pressing her down, Rosie could feel herself getting excited. Her breasts tingled and the same feeling she got between her legs whenever she and Eddie kissed was present and aching. The director kept the action going, as the tension on the set became palpable. *Click-click-click* worked the camera crank as Gray's passion heightened. With Louise's arms tight around his neck, they locked lips in a long, passionate kiss.

We can hear a pin drop. She ogled the scene, riveted. Then, sneaking a glance over at Eddie, she saw he was gazing at her from across the room.

Because of Gertie's insistence that they end the day with a few swigs from Clara's flask, Rosie was more than a little tipsy as she slowly made her way over to Eddie's and her secret hideout—a large, industrial janitor's mop and broom closet. Opened every night at eight, completely overlooked during the day, Eddie had gotten a hold of the key and managed to make two extra copies. Unromantic, yet practical, it served them well as a quiet getaway from the frenetic goings-on all around them.

Swaying slightly, Rosie approached the door and fumbled with the lock. Eddie, already inside, opened it up for her, flashing a huge grin.

He kissed her lightly on the cheek. "I've got great news."

"Oh?" She was having trouble focusing on his face.

"I spoke to Lon Chaney, and he wants to meet you. How about dinner at his place next week?"

"Sure. Can we see his studio?"

"Of course. Just wait until you see it! Such great makeup and special effects. Rosie? You okay?"

She pressed against him, and as soon as she put her arms around his neck, she uplifted her lips for a long, deeper than usual kiss.

He kissed her back, then pulled away slightly. He chuckled. "Have we been drinking?"

"Perhaps." She uplifted her lips again, back for more pleasure. Revved up from an afternoon of watching passion, she could feel a new urgency within her, stronger than ever before.

"Oh, Rosie, Rosie." He half groaned and kissed her back again, this time with the full weight of his body against her, bending her backward over a stack of cartons.

She could feel herself swirling toward an abyss, slowly, deliciously, a sudden wave of intensity enveloping her. Images of Eddie, bare-chested like she had once seen him on a blistering summer's day on the set, now seeped into her brain like a runaway carousel, circling around and around, as she grew more and more ardent, throbbing for some kind of release.

"Oh, Rosie, oh God, you slay me. But we should stop." Eddie's deep, guttural voice finally broke through.

"Why?" she moaned, her yellow lipstick smeared beyond her lips. "I'm ready, I'm ready now."

He stepped back, his heavy breathing filling the room. When he finally spoke, his tone was husky. "Look, sweetheart, I want this as much as you. But not here, not now. When we do make love, it will be in a proper bed, with music playing and candles glowing."

She placed her hand over her quaking chest and tried to breathe. *A fine time to be such a romantic gentleman.*

Taking her hand, he led her over to the door. "Rosie, listen. I don't mean to be a wet blanket. I just think you deserve better than a quickie, as they say. And certainly not surrounded by mops and brooms." He put his arm around her and gave her a gentle hug. "I think I better take you take you home now."

Their ride back to the Highland Courts was oddly quiet. No easy banter, none of their typical laughter, just an unspoken heaviness between them that to him, was unbearable. Was Rosie angry or embarrassed? Eddie wondered. He tried a couple of times to ask her but her only response was a dismissive wave and a sudden interest in what was rolling by her window.

Pulling up to the courts' curb, he got out to come around and open up her door, but she was already standing out on the pathway, looking away. Yet, when she let him take her arm, relief flooded through him.

"Rosie, please. You have to understand, my actions had nothing to do with how much I wanted you, but because I care for you so much."

She nodded and stroked his arm lightly, a faraway look on her face.

Good, maybe she's forgiven me. Just as she turned to go into her apartment, she swiveled around to face him.

"Eddie, it's all right. I'm just confused. I..."

She got no further. Walt had walked out and positioned himself against the archway. "Your mother wants you inside, Rosie," he called out.

She went inside, and as the older man walked down the steps and past the carpenter, Eddie could hear what sounded like panting.

Just like a faithful dog. Back in his car, Eddie drove home.

January 5, 1926
One Day AFTER the Harris Shooting

As he drove past Medford Studios, Frank noticed Pete Roberts exiting the giant gates. Slamming on his brakes, the detective careened over to the curb, got out of the car, and approached the cameraman.

"Ah, a moment of your time, Roberts," he said. He was met with open hostility.

"Now what, detective?"

"I wanted to go over your relationship with Harris, is all."

Robert's laughter was more of a snort than anything else. "Why in the world would you be wasting your time on me? You need to check out Henry Blake. He knew his boss well enough to know Harris owed the mob and the City Hall Gang plenty of money. Why don't you ask *him* what he was doing two nights before the murder?"

"What do you mean?" *Is this the moment when something big's gonna open up?*

"I mean, I ran into Blake that night. He was with some guy who looked like he was maybe connected to the City Hall Gang. It seemed like a kind of payoff."

"Why did you say he was probably from the City Hall Gang?" Frank was almost in Robert's face.

The cameraman stepped back a pace. "Because the man was dressed in a good suit and Fedora hat. And he didn't look like you, detective."

"What the hell does that mean?"

"You know, a gumbah. No offense, detective."

Frank let out a low growl. *Enough of the Italian slurs.*

Roberts continued. "Anyway, Blake was handing over a nice, big, fat envelope to him, and I don't think it was a greeting card, if you know what I mean. Can I please go now, detective?"

Frank nodded absently. This is a whole different ball game. He felt a chill. *God knows what will happen if I now have to start circling crooked politicians. And the mob.*

January 6, 1926
Two Days AFTER the Harris Shooting

Frank studied Henry Blake sitting across from him. Dapper, impeccably dressed, the slender man had, once again, carried with him the smell of men's cologne, which wafted up and out all around them in the police interview room. Frank had already figured he was probably one of those "sissies." But today, the detective attempted to appear neutral and not let his prejudices show. It must have worked because Blake quickly opened up.

"Detective, I'll bet the mob did this to my boss. It makes sense. Chester Harris was up to his eyeballs with loan debt to the Ardizzone gang, you know," he said, his chin jutted out.

Pretty smug. Particularly after two witnesses had come forward the day before to recount the harsh dialogue between Harris and Blake up at the Villa Capistrano. According to both of them, that was a scant two weeks before the killing. Then there was Pete Robert's eye-witness account.

The detective had asked the two men where the villa was located, and the smirks and side-glances told him instantly about the sort of men probably included on the guest list.

Frank pulled himself back to the present and Henry Blake. "So, you worked with Mr. Harris, correct?"

Henry cleared his throat. "Yes, detective, and it was a privilege to do so."

Frank fought back a snort. *Privilege, my ass.* His mind filled with the other men's sworn testimony that Blake had had nothing but lethal things to say about his boss for two whole weeks after the incident at that party. Apparently, he ranted about how much he hated Harris and would get even with him one day.

That was enough for Frank. Blake was definitely a suspect, and from Pete's tip the day before, the mob, along with Kane and Parrot—the dirty boys up in City Hall—might very well have played a hand in this whole thing. Word around town was beginning to become clear: there was a ninety-five to one chance Harris had been doomed. He had obviously picked the wrong guys to do business with. And not pay his debts? That was plain suicide. The head of the mobsters, Joseph "Iron Man" Ardizzone didn't fool around when it came to money. *I'll bet money the Harris shooting had nothing to do with the other two shootings.*

That evening, the detective took a long walk to clear his head. It was a slow amble past neighborhood shops closing up tight for the night. People were hurrying home, and the filled-to-the-gills trolley cars rattled and clanged their steady way along each assigned route.

Something is not right about Henry Blake. The man's definitely not telling me everything. Not even close.

Once home, he immediately got out his bottle of whiskey, and after several slugs of booze, in spite of his normal desire to investigate this and any case fully, he kept rolling back to the same, nagging question: How do I stop this urge to just blame Eddie Willis?

January 7, 1926
Three Days AFTER the Harris Shooting

As soon as Frank stepped into police headquarters the next morning at ten-thirty, he was reminded of his youth. In 1896, newly immigrated from Italy and dirt poor, he and his family had joined relatives in Paterson, New Jersey, where the factories' endless outlay of a thick, gray haze was a daily occurrence.

Here, amongst his fellow officers, clouds of choking cigarette smoke accosted him, dimming his vision and making breathing more than a little difficult. *Good Lord, we've all gotta stop buying them cigs.* He made his way over to the cluttered, two-sided desk he shared with Detective Shire. For more than five years, the two had been partners, and to a certain extent, friends. Shoptalk together over drinks a couple of times a week at their secret bar, Smarty's, was their habit. For Frank, that signified friendship. He had learned from experience, anything more usually didn't work out very well.

He nodded to his partner who was immersed in both paperwork and swilling down the department's barely tolerable coffee.

Shire looked up. "Coming in a little late, aren't we?" He smirked.

One of the secretaries approached. "Coffee, Detective Lozano?" she asked flirtatiously. She put her thin, lizard-like hand up near her high collar and patted it.

Shire chuckled slightly, but Frank simply nodded, blinking against the thick air. "Thanks, Beth. That'd be swell." He knew he should have smiled at her. After all, she was one of the few people in there besides Shire who actually liked him. But he was beat-tired. And discouraged. Eddie Willis was probably not the shooter. *Would that put Rosie out of reach for good?* He sighed.

Out of the corner of his eye, he picked up Harris' stepsister, Sheila Morgan, talking animatedly to one of the other detectives. She was obviously being palmed off on one cop after another. *Oh, brother, her again.* He held his head, which felt as if it was about to explode.

"Listen up, listen up," Captain Billings called out as he strode into the room. "We got ourselves our first clue." He took a spent bullet casing out of a paper bag with tweezers. "This here is a casing shell from the shooter's rooftop. It was definitely from a 1903 Springfield bolt-action rifle. Most probably with a scope." He dropped it back into the bag and looked over at Frank.

"Detective Lozano. In my office. Now."

Frank, his pulse suddenly accelerated, got up, and followed his boss. *Now I can get rid of Willis.* The swell of male voices filled the room behind him. *I'll tell the captain about the carpenter's rifle. Yeah, that's the ticket.*

Inside the sergeant's office, Billings was direct. "You never told me how the questioning of that sissy movie fellow went yesterday. I assume your absence this morning means you've been working on it today. Anything there?"

"I didn't think so, but now I do. There's someone else I think is more of a person of interest than Henry Blake. His name is Eddie Willis, a jack-of-all trades kind of guy on the movie sets, who also owns a similar rifle like the one you just talked about."

"Why the *hell* didn't you mention this before, detective?"

"It held no gun residue. But now, I'm thinking that since this guy is supposed to be, as they say, 'resourceful,' why couldn't he have cleaned it up good?"

"Hmm. Resourceful." Billings seemed deep in thought. "That would also explain something else they found that I didn't mention to the rest of the officers."

"Yeah? What?"

"Apparently, there were no foot prints up on the roof, just odd, parallel smudges across it."

"What does *that* mean?"

"It means someone was clever enough to think of using some kind of fabric to camouflage his shoe tracks."

Someone who helps create different characters with all of their clothing accessories. Suddenly, Lon Chaney's assistant loomed much larger than he had before. Eddie would surely have access to the man's studio. And to fabric.

"Anyway, you want to go higher on the ladder around here, Lozano? This is your chance. Just don't disappoint me. Remember, we need to find the killer *now*, no matter what, no matter who." He mumbled something about Medford and two other names—Crawford and Parrot.

"Crawford and Parrot, sir?" Frank asked. *Here we go, the City Hall Gang leaders. Crooked as bent twigs.*

Billings looked slightly jarred. "No, not them. I meant just those damn studio executives from Medford. They're still pressuring me, Lozano, to come up with anyone so they can move on. I promised them I would oblige."

Frank grimaced. "Sure." The irony of that statement was not lost on him. Outside in the main room, the amount of open graft between the police and the studios had been up and running for well over three years. And as for Crawford and Parrot? Everyone knew they both had started the corrupt City Hall Gang. But just how deep was Billings involved with them? *Odds are he's on the take himself.*

As soon as Frank plunked down at his desk, he looked over at his partner. "Hey..." he started, then stopped.

Two detectives near them were laughing as they exchanged a thick, padded envelope. A wad of paper bills, he surmised. Leaning back in his chair, he cupped his hands behind his head and studied them. Concentrating, he thought he heard the name "Crawford and Medford" mentioned together a couple of times. A minute later, another officer joined them.

"Hey, count me in. I could sure use a new car," he said loudly. All three of them cackled. Until they caught sight of Frank.

"What you staring at, Lozano?" one of them quipped. "Never seen grown men actually having a good time?"

Frank's jaw clenched. "All's I see is you guys don't give a damn about solving a murder. A man recently got shot in cold blood, remember?"

In the background, he could hear his partner softly muttering, "Give it up, Frank. It ain't worth it."

He ignored Shire.

"Yeah, yeah, Lozano. Save it for your epitaph." All three snickered in unison.

"I don't know why you even bother, Frank," Shire said. "Around here your honesty might save your soul, but not your career. How 'bout some relaxation? Smarty's after work? That is, if you can handle any more drinking. You think I don't know that's why you came in late today?"

Frank chugged down some more burnt coffee. "Sure," he said. "Smarty's, it is."

No one seemed to question why there was always a slow, steady stream of customers entering Mario's Funeral Parlor, all hours of the day. And most of the night. Whether it be the parlor's front entrance, side access, or its back-alley door, most everyone who came in ended up at the same destination inside: Smarty's.

The funeral parlor in and of itself was nothing unusual. Various coffins of differing wood and quality were placed on pedestals throughout a large, flower-filled room. Around-the-clock music floated out from an Internal Horn Victrola, courtesy of someone named George, who cranked its handle nonstop. It was the perfect atmosphere for those wishing to send their loved ones off to heaven with dignity and beauty.

A small door toward the back of the coffin room was a different story. Once opened, recordings of Louis Armstrong, Jelly Roll Morton, or live, hot jazz gave any incoming patron more than a hint of what lurked beyond.

A short walk through a twisting, maze-like corridor brought customers to the main attraction—an even larger room, where a well-worn mahogany bar took up the length of one wall. Twenty barstools encircled the bar, and twelve nearby tables were usually packed, especially at night. In one corner, there was a thrown together, slap-dash stage, big enough for a trio at best, and in front of that, a small dance floor for customers to either fast jitter-bug or dance the Charleston.

Frank spied Shire across the room, sitting on a barstool, hunched over in his typical gin-guzzling position. After the detective sat down next to his drunk, "half-overseas" partner, he nodded to the bartender. Immediately, a shot glass filled with whiskey was placed in front of him.

"I sure could use this," Frank muttered. Before he took his first gulp, he rapped twice on the bar. He downed the whiskey in two seconds and started on the new glass the bartender quickly placed before him.

"I keep tellin' you, you take office politics too hard, Frank," Shire said, his words already slurred.

"Doesn't it bother you how corrupt the police force—hell, the entire city government—is?"

Shire shrugged. "Of course, it does." He hiccupped and motioned another round to the bartender. "I just have my own way of dealing with it."

"Well, I'm sick of it. Sick of those wind suckers." Frank guzzled his second glass of whisky. "You got any cigs handy?"

Shire chugged down his glass. "Wind suckers, huh? Why wouldn't they brag their heads off? They're making good money, ain't they? Tell me something new, Lozano. I'm getting tired of the same conversation. And by the way, don't be such a grubber. Next time bring your own damn cigarettes!"

Frank rapped again on the bar, waited for the bartender to fulfill his duty, then held up his refresher glass in the light, as if examining artwork in a museum.

"Something new, huh? Okay, try this one on for size." He slugged back the whiskey and put the glass down with a clunk. "I met an angel the other day."

With one eye closed, Shire stared at him. "Come again?"

"An angel. This girl I met on the Harris murder set. Rosie Paige is her name. She makes me wish I'd met her in my younger days. I think I'm in love."

"Now don't go all goofy on this girl. It's lust. You're in lust with her.

That's not a good sign. If I were a gambling man, I sure as hell wouldn't bet on your track record in that area, especially when it comes to dames. Remember how it all started with your wife, Susannah—marriage, kids, the whole shebang. And look where that ended up. By the way, how are those kids of yours? Hmm?"

"Nice," Frank mumbled. "Don't you dare raze me. You ain't got such a great record in that department either."

"Maybe so. But come on, you've told me yourself how you ain't good at picking them. Remember after the Christmas party, and you went home with that dame, the one with the long, shapely gams. What was her name again?"

"Bertha."

"Yeah, Bertha, that's the one."

"This one's different. I can feel it in my gut. I've gone out with plenty of gals where nobody's home. Not this girl. She's got spunk, and she's a real looker. The only problem is—"

"Oh, boy." Shire chuckled. "Let's hear it."

"She might have a boyfriend. And at this point, he's supposed to be the lead suspect in the case."

Laughing, Shire slapped his right knee. "Now that's rich! Good luck to you on that one." He paused. "Wait a minute. What the hell do you mean by 'supposed' to be?"

"Billings needs someone, and I've been thinking, that if this boyfriend goes to jail, then he won't be a problem with Rosie, now, will he?"

Shire's face sobered in an instant. "Watch it, detective. Remember, you're supposed to be the honest one."

With a loud huff, Frank stood up. "Gotta go."

"Where to?"

"To question someone." When Frank palmed down his money, he avoided his partner's eyes.

Once again, he parked in front of the Highland Courts. Only this time, he had a definite purpose. Or at least, that's what he told himself. On the walkway up to the main archway, he paused. The night air was mild, the bushes around the apartment complex fragrant, and if he concentrated hard enough, he figured he'd be able to act normal, no matter how much his head was beginning to spin.

When he knocked on the Paige's front door, he could hear movement inside. With his hand, he made a fast, last second comb through of his dark, wavy hair, then straightened his twisted tie.

She answered the door. *Zowie.* She was obviously going out on the town. All dressed up, perfect makeup, she was like a vision. *Angel, hell.* He wanted to scoop her up and…

"Detective Lozano, isn't it?"

He nodded and gulped. *Smooth, Frank, smooth.*

"What are you doing here? And at night. Is there a problem?"

Was that a twitch of a smile at the corners of her mouth? And those lips. Perfect for kissing.

He gulped again. *Think man, think.*

That wasn't happening, so he willed himself into detective mode. Taking out his pad and pencil, he managed, "Sorry for the late hour. A detective's job is never done."

"Where'd you get that line from? The Police Detective handbook?"

He laughed in spite of himself. "Hah, nice one, Miss Paige."

"Do you want to come in, detective?"

Was it his imagination or was she radiating some physical attraction toward him? He was definitely out of practice, so he couldn't be sure. Still, his pulse had begun to climb.

She led him into the living room, where an older woman was sitting on a sofa, with several magazines spread out next to her. At first glance, they appeared to be those movie rags. *Total junk.* Still, he nodded to her and removed his hat.

"Mama, this here is Detective Lozano from the Los Angeles' police," Rosie said.

"Oh?" Beatrice eyes widened.

"Remember, about the murder of the producer, Chester Harris?" She turned to Frank. "Any new leads, detective?"

"Possibly." *If she only knew.*

She smiled. "Anyone I know, or is that question not allowed?" She pursed her lips together then retracted them.

Is she flirting with me? He wished he knew. Meantime, his heartbeat was going double time, along with another part of his anatomy. *Her mother's here, you lunatic.* His head swirling, he resisted the urge to put his hand against a wall to steady himself.

"So, what questions do you have for me, detective?" Even all dolled up, she looked so innocent, so sweet.

He suddenly realized the problem with spontaneity. And whisky. Had he thought this one through, he could have done this visit far better. He cleared his throat. "I've been asking people to see if there was anything they might have forgotten about that day." *Good job, Frank.*

"I don't know. I don't think there is anything else I could add."

Did she really put her hand on her chest just now and stroke it slightly? Suddenly, he wondered where he could go with her. In private.

"Well, for example, your friend, what's his name again?"

"Eddie. Eddie Willis."

"Yes, that's him. Seems he wasn't there when it happened. Could you tell me…"

He stopped. Her face had completely shut down.

You fool. You ruined it.

He opened his mouth, then shut it tight when the sudden knock on the door sounded like a loud drumbeat.

No longer smiling, she strode past him to open it. He could hear the sound of a quick kiss, and then Eddie's voice. "Here, I brought you these for Ginger and Patches." Then came a small laugh from her before she and Eddie entered the living room together.

Damn. Frank steadied himself.

"Eddie, you remember Detective Lozano, don't you?" Rosie asked.

"How could I forget?" Eddie muttered.

"I better be going," Frank said. He nodded to Beatrice and headed for the door. As he passed Eddie, his next words came out more like a low growl. "Don't leave town."

Eddie snapped around. "Look, if you're gonna arrest me, you'd better have a good reason."

Frank noticed Eddie's arm was resting casually over Rosie's shoulders.

"Oh, I got plenty," he said and walked out the door, his head feeling like it was about to explode.

As he approached his car, he noticed on the lawn, off to one side, there was a small Colgate tooth powder can—red, white, and abandoned. He took it in only peripherally, like an obscure wall hanging at a crime scene. He made it to his car, pushed the starter, and after several sloppy hand cranks, he stumbled back over to his car door and slid in. Pausing, he leaned his head against the seatback and closed his eyes.

Damn. Damn.

Suddenly, he thrust the door open with his foot, got out, and charged over to the tooth powder can. With a loud grunt, he kicked it so hard it flew up into the air and careened across the street into a neighbor's front yard.

Back in the car, with the gear positioned in forward, he shoved his accelerator foot all the way to the floor.

December 30, 1925
Five Days BEFORE the Harris Shooting

In truth, Alonzo wasn't that happy. Oh, he liked the target practice Ardizzone and his cousin Tony had set up just fine. In fact, he relished it—loved feeling the power and precision involved. He just wished he had had this ability way back, when he was stuck in that hellhole they called an orphanage. How sweet it would have been to blip off at least one of those evil supervisors who made his young life a relentless nightmare.

He shrugged. *Spilt milk.* Still, getting this new assignment made him feel a bit uneasy. But according to Tony, gunning down a man Alonzo didn't even know meant the big time with better money to come. Besides that, the firing position that Ardizzone's men had set up for the lad was a simple shot. The industrial warehouse's rooftop near the main outdoor Medford set was a lot closer in range than the distances Alonzo was now shooting from. Piece of cake, really.

"This is the big time, cousin," Tony had told him, and that was probably true. Already, he had noticed Ardizzone's nods in passing had turned into winks. No doubt about it—he was "in."

When his first set of instructions came, it was also via Tony—short and to the point. "Alonzo, after the studio sends out its filming schedule for the week, I'll notify you. Your job, then, will be to make sure you're up on the roof, ready to go at the appointed time. And be sure not to leave any footprints." Tony placed a hand on his cousin's shoulder. "This is straight from Ardizzone himself. What do you say?"

Alonzo shrugged.

"Hey, look," Tony said, "I know the first one's always the hardest. We've all been there, kid. So, all's you have to do is concentrate on your target and squeeze that trigger. You can do it. Why, if two of Ardizzone's new recruits were able to knock off two nobodies—one a couple of years ago, another one, just a year ago—and not get caught, believe me, you can do it. But Ardizzone's got your back. In fact, he told me just recently how much faith he has in you. That's why you get to off a hotshot producer. What do ya say?"

Alonzo swallowed hard. "I say I'm ready to go, Tony."

CHAPTER SEVEN

"Between pictures, there is no Lon Chaney."
— Lon Chaney, actor and makeup artist wizard

January 11, 1926
Seven Days AFTER the Harris Shooting

"NEVER LET IT be said that Rosie can't experience the finest of things in life," Beatrice was fond of saying.

As Rosie took her position on the set of the famous author, F. Scott Fitzgerald's *The Great Gatsby*, she suddenly thought of that constant line of her mother's and chuckled. *Mama, does making this movie based on the best-selling author's newest novel qualify as one of the finer things in life?* Knowing her mother's taste in literature, she figured most probably not.

The actor, William Powell, was there, as well as a very debonair Warner Baxter, who lounged off to one side. He was chatting with one of the female leads, Lois Wilson, as they all waited for directions.

The director, Herbert Brenon, stepped forward to call out, "Places, everyone, places. Extras, over to stage left and take your marks. And William, Warner, Lois? Ready?"

As he announced, "Take one," Rosie noticed a well-tailored, middle-age man sitting in a chair, staring at her from across the set.

She took her place, and, as was specified to her, tried to emote a look of gaiety. She listened for the director's yell of "Cut!"

It came quickly.

"Sorry, people. Lois' makeup needs a little touch up."

From behind a column, out stepped Eddie to hand a large makeup case over to Miss Wilson. As he stood there waiting for her to apply the greasepaint, he winked at Rosie, then made their special signal.

She nodded, grinning. When he returned to his station, something made her glance across the set. Again, the dapper-looking gentleman was eyeing her.

The shoot continued until the final "cut and print" was announced. Quickly, Rosie picked up her own makeup kit to meet up with Eddie.

A young man approached her. "Excuse me, Miss Paige, Mr. Berns would like to speak to you."

Her head cocked slightly. Berns? Suddenly, she remembered what one of the girls had told her about him. "He's an all right sort, better than a lot of them."

The man pointed to the classy, well-dressed man. "He's a producer." He leaned in close, and with a hand cupped around his mouth, muttered, "He's one of the big ones, Miss. If I was you, I would see what he has to say."

Shrugging, she followed him over to Berns, who immediately stood up and gallantly took her hand. "I've been checking on you, m'dear. You have, shall we say, a quality."

"Thank you. I guess." She noticed Eddie over toward the exit, looking tense.

The producer followed her gaze, then cleared his throat. "Frankly, I think you could go far. I should like to take you out for dinner. Shall we say this Friday night?"

"I don't know." Again, she glanced over at Eddie.

"I certainly mean no disrespect, Miss Paige. I simply want to discuss business, and why not over dinner? My driver and I can pick you up. Let's say seven o'clock? I will get your address from the studio."

He leaned in an inch. "Well?"

She nodded, thinking of her mother's glee. "I suppose so."

"Perfect. Friday night it is." He smiled. "And Miss Paige, do wear something nice. I'll be taking you to a brand-new restaurant called the Brown Derby on Wilshire Boulevard. You never know how many stars might show up."

Won't Mama be fit to be tied. She hurried toward Eddie's and her special spot. As she made double time, cameras, film stands, and a few props were being transported back to the main storeroom. Actors and actresses were heading either to the back parking lot or the front entrance, to catch the five-fifteen trolley.

Ignoring everyone around her, she picked up her pace as she waffled between wanting to please her mother and finding out why Eddie looked so upset. Suddenly, she saw him up ahead, sitting on a wooden bench just shy of their special hideaway.

"I don't trust that Berns' guy," he growled as she approached him.

"Why are you sitting here?" she asked.

"You know I like to see the backdrops roll by at the end of the day. Did you hear what I said?"

She shrugged. "One of the girls said he's all right, one of the good ones."

"Hmm." Eddie's growl grew deeper.

"I can take care of myself, you know. It's just for dinner, Eddie. He says he wants to discuss business. Besides, if you must know, I'm really doing this for my mother."

"I figured as much. I've known you for a year now, and I can tell that all the glamorous stuff doesn't get you all goofy, like a lot of the other girls. Or, as some of the guys call them, 'tomatoes.'"

Laughing, she joined him on the bench.

"That's what I like about you, Rosie," he said. "You're smart." Within seconds, his arms went around her waist, and his lips nibbled on her neck.

Gooseflesh rippled up and down her arms as she slowly turned her head to offer him her lips.

He took his cue and met her in a soft kiss. Out of the corner of her eye, Rosie could see a couple of actresses stroll by, giggling at them. Still, her lips remained locked with his.

"Hey, Eddie Willis, get a hotel room, why don't cha?" a set-builder called out, walking in step to a large piece of scenery of the famous Versailles of France rolling by.

They separated, leaned against the bench back, and let their deep breaths slowly dissipate, while a giant California countryside background painting trundled by.

He took her hand. "That scene really reminds me of my hometown. My father used to take me camping up in the hills around us. It was magical, with the campfire, the sky filled with stars. Someday, maybe I'll go back and open up a car shop with my father. He's always been such a great guy."

"Lucky you," she muttered.

He sighed softly. "Rosie, I didn't mean to…"

"I know, I know. I'm glad you had it so good with your folks. Truly, I am. It's just that when you grow up with a father who left when you were so young and a mother who's never gonna forgive him, I sometimes wonder how my life would have turned out if I had had your parents, you know?"

He gave a little chuckle. "Thank goodness you didn't. We'd be brother and sister. Ouch!"

She nodded, the hint of a smile beginning, then instantly fading. "Mama was so destroyed at first. I knew they weren't getting along. It only took one thing to convince me of that—his ducking at her flying hairbrush." She sat still, her eyes growing moist. "No. It just broke my heart to see how depressed she got after he was gone. Never getting off the couch for days on end, not even washing herself or our dishes. It was so awful." She blinked back her oncoming tears. "You know what snapped her out of it?"

He shook his head, his arms around her again.

"She saw Valentino in *The Sheik*, and the world of Hollywood gave her hope. As she told me many times, particularly as I grew older, if not for her, then for me."

"Hollywood. Hope? That's a good one. I bet even your Walt would agree to that."

"The Rosie-Posey man?" she said, laughing.

"What do you mean?"

"That's Walt's nickname for me. He says it all the time. It's a cute rhyme, don't you think?"

"Sure." He paused for several seconds. "Seriously, Rosie, there are four things to remember."

She leaned against his shoulder.

"One, I think your Mama needs to see the world in more than just Hollywood colors. Maybe there's a different rainbow out there just waiting for you."

"And two?"

"Second, no matter what, you've gotta watch the sharks in Hollywood. I mean sharks like that Berns. I haven't heard such great things about him, by the way."

She held up three fingers.

"Three, stop fighting your need to always please your mother. If we got married, I would take care of you, and you could do whatever you wanted." He paused. "And I'd take care of your mother, too, for that matter. If she'll let me."

She said nothing. The image of Beatrice glowering overtook any words.

Another scene rattled by, this time, a painting of a nighttime city street. He stroked her arm casually as together they looked on to see the sun beginning its slow, downward arc.

She showed him four fingers, a faint smile stretching the corners of her mouth.

"Four, are you ready to go to Lon's later tonight for dinner? I can't wait for you two to meet. Come, I'll take you home so you can change out of your costume cocktail dress. Lon's is definitely casual."

Their hands intertwined, Eddie and Rosie hastened up the narrow brick pathway leading to Lon Chaney's home. She could just feel Eddie's excitement. After months of talking to her about his older friend, his mentor, she was finally going to meet the man. Yet when first they had parked in front of the small, cottage-style house, she was taken by surprise. Why wasn't his house bigger, more elaborate? After all, he was now the world's greatest makeup artist. A true genius, everyone agreed. Certainly, he could afford something grander, more eye-catching, couldn't he? Eddie had driven her past Gloria Swanson's house, as well as Louise Brook's, and just viewing both of their mansions, she assumed most movie celebrities would automatically require the same stature for themselves.

"Lon Chaney's not like the rest of them," Eddie had explained when she voiced her opinion. His tone definitely sounded defensive, and in a split second, she realized her faux pas. For Eddie, the subject of Chaney was obviously sacred ground.

Several knocks, and the door opened wide. Not by a servant, but by Lon Chaney himself, his chiseled face lit up with a tremendous smile.

"Dear Eddie, welcome." He gave his protégé a warm hug. Then, he turned and bowed slightly to Rosie. "And this must be the famous Miss Paige.

Glad you could come."

She laughed and stretched out her hand. "Don't know about the famous part, but thank you for inviting me, Mr. Chaney. It's indeed a great honor. And please, do call me Rosie."

"And you, my dear, must call me Lon. We don't stand on ceremony around here, do we, Eddie?"

"Not at all," Eddie said. He grinned at a petite, attractive woman entering the small front vestibule, with two dogs walking behind her, their tails drooping down.

Clapping her hands in delight, Rosie sank down onto the floor with the canines. Instantly, the dogs came alive. They leapt onto her and took turns licking her face, barking and running around her, as their tails swatted back and forth so hard, they looked as if they might break off.

The woman tried to calm them down. "My goodness. I don't know what's gotten into them. They *never* behave like this with strangers. Stop it, fellas! She's our guest."

"It's all right. I love it!" Rosie exclaimed. Both dogs attacked her all at once with wet doggie kisses. She fell over backward, convulsed with laughter.

Lon immediately ran over to her. "You all right, Rosie?"

Eddie laughed. "That's my girl. She's in heaven, Lon, don't worry."

"Seems like we should get her off the floor, though, don't you agree, Eddie?" the woman directed.

Nodding, Eddie extended his hand to Rosie, who grabbed it and let him pull her up into a standing position.

The dogs tried to leap onto her again, but with a sharp, "Heel!" from Lon, they backed off, and resorted to muted, wistful whimpers.

"Rosie, I'd like you meet Hazel," Lon said. "Hazel, Rosie."

Hazel giggled. "Well, we all know what you like, Rosie. My, that was certainly a first for our boys here."

Everyone laughed as Lon guided them all into a charming, old-style living room, where a welcoming fire rendered a soft, cozy sheen to the room with its overstuffed floral sofas, armchairs, and beige walls. The dogs were allowed in as well, but with one low warning from Lon. They gathered around Rosie and draped themselves over her shoes, their tails thumping slowly against the floor.

"All right, Rosie?" Hazel asked with a worried look.

Rosie laughed. "More than all right!"

"Let's everyone have their cocktails before we eat, shall we?" Lon motioned his guests to sit while he made his way over to an antique cabinet, on top of which sat three bottles—gin, vermouth, and whisky. Like soldiers standing in rapt attention, the bottles stood in formation next to a cocktail shaker and four delicate glasses. Within minutes, "Gin-Rickies" and "Sidecars" intermingled with nonstop, flowing conversation about life in Los Angeles, the beauty of its weather, and all its fine scenery.

Suddenly Hazel asked, "Rosie, have you always loved dogs?"

"Yes, I have. All animals, actually."

Eddie laughed. "I can vouch for that. I found this out on our third date."

"Do tell," Hazel urged.

Nodding, he began. "It happened on a summer's evening at five o'clock, as we were driving along at a steady clip, enjoying talking about this or that. I didn't even notice a lump laying on the side of the road. But Rosie sure did. 'Stop the car, Eddie, stop the car!' she said. So, I swerved my Tin Lizzy over to the side of the road and stopped. 'What in the world?' I remember saying.

"But Rosie was already out of the car and running back to a strange looking object that, from a distance seemed like an old, rumpled coat. With the car still running, I climbed out and hurried over to her.

"'Look, it's a dog. He's hurt. We've *got* to get him help, Eddie,' she said." He stopped.

At this point, Lon and Hazel both smiled at Rosie. "Go on, Eddie," Lon said.

Eddie continued. "I remember looking down at the mangy creature and shaking my head. 'I don't know, Rosie. I think he's had it.' Boy, I'll never forget the look on her face. Determination, fury, and panic gave her a force I hadn't seen in her before. It was, well, riveting.

"'He's still alive' she said. 'Help me get him into the car! We can go to Dr. Peterson, the veterinarian I use for my cat, Ginger.'"

Lon and his wife sat still, in rapt attention as Eddie talked about the kind veterinarian who immediately took the dog in and fixed him up. Then later, when the vet talked about Rosie's abilities, he said he would hire her if he could. Meantime, she should take the dog—with his blessing.

When Eddie finished, Hazel blinked back a couple of tears.

Lon cleared his throat. "Lovely story, Eddie." He turned to Rosie. "Maybe you should work with animals, Rosie." He paused. "I think it's time for us all to go have some supper, don't you?" He stood up and offered Rosie his arm.

At the dinner table, amidst candles and home-cooked food, their talkfest soon turned to how Lon and Eddie first met.

"All I can tell you, Rosie, is there is much chance in life. Case in point? The first time I met Eddie." Lon looked over at his protégé. "Remember, Eddie?"

Eddie chuckled. "How could I forget? I remember it well. It was up in Fillmore, my hometown, in the middle of summer. July, I think."

Lon nodded, his face taking on a faraway expression. "I remember back then how the heat had gotten to both me and my car. It was at Eddie's father's little roadside gas station, called Willis Gasoline. A single pump, no real garage in sight. Not much to it, as I recall."

"Nope, it sure wasn't." Eddie nodded.

"But there was also a young girl there, a friend of yours, I believe. What was her name? She was sweet. Still friends?" Lon asked.

Eddie's face changed dramatically. "Her name was Maggie Luther, and no, we lost touch." There was a long pause.

She saw Lon and Hazel exchange looks *Wonder what that's about?*

"And there you were beside your father," Lon continued, "bending underneath my hood, and like a chemistry professor, you examined the evidence as the steam hissed and puttered from my engine. I can still picture your face. You looked so concerned, as if it was your friend needing to go to the hospital."

The lopsided grin on Eddie's face tickled Rosie. *This is going to be interesting.*

"Yes," Lon continued. "Your father thought it might be a cracked engine block, which would have cost me a bundle. But you shook your head, remember?"

"I do, indeed." Eddie gave an exaggerated shrug. "Let's just say my dad was a better salesman than a mechanic." He paused. "But he sure loved that place. Killed him to have to sell it, all because after I left, some customers dropped off."

"I hope you don't blame yourself for that, Eddie," Lon said.

"Not really, although sometimes I wonder."

"Wonder what?" Rosie asked, a sudden fear cropping up. Was he going to leave her too, so he could return to help his father? "So, what happened next?" she asked, her fingers intertwined.

"Well, Rosie, Eddie ignored his father and said straight out that it was simply a water hose break, and he could fix it right away. At no cost, as I recall."

Rosie smiled. "An honest man, to be sure."

"Yes, he certainly impressed me. Remember, Eddie, what I told you later, in private?"

"Of course. You said, 'Here is my card, kid. Any time you wanna try your hand in Hollywood, just look me up. I'll get you a job.' And, as they say, the rest is history."

"No matter how it happened, we're both so glad you're here," Hazel piped in.

Suddenly, Lon looked serious. "Yes, unlike some people I've known, you've got yourself a good man, Rosie. A diamond in the rough."

As conversation resumed, Rosie studied the man she had been dating for almost a year. Even in casual, loose-fitting clothes, his body could not be hidden. Whenever he reached over to pour more water into people's glasses, she could see the definition of his strong, muscular arms pressed against his shirt. When he got up to help Hazel bring in the dessert, his thighs, his buttocks gave hints to their shape and firmness. *Handsome and kind.* He probably wouldn't leave her like her father left her mother, would he? Suddenly, Mark Oliver and Willy Sweet slipped into her thoughts. *Wonder what I did to make them both so disinterested? Was I that unworthy?*

"Lon, I was wondering if you could show us your studio," Eddie said. "I know Rosie would love to see it."

Lon nodded and tossed his napkin onto the table. "Let's go then, shall we?"

En masse, they followed him toward the back of the house and his sprawling studio, where the first thing that struck Rosie's interest was his array of masks. Carefully displayed together in a wide glass case, each face was turned forward, with expressions that ranged from anger, confusion, and a clown's sadness, to terror, surprise, and embarrassment.

Like a Greek chorus, cheering him on? She examined each one carefully.

"Do they have names?" she asked.

Lon burst out laughing. "No, honey, they don't. How about you naming them?"

She cocked her head. "Hmm. Let's see. Maybe the clown mask is Bill, the angry mask, Hildegarde, and the embarrassed mask, Augustus."

They all laughed.

"I guess that's good enough for starters." Lon winked at her. "Quite a gal you got there, Eddie."

Next came the meat and potatoes of his work. A large, wooden, four-tiered makeup box, which, when opened, displayed tubes of grease paint, assorted false teeth, and gray Plasticine, molded into a mixture of noses—wide, large, small, and upturned.

"Rosie, you gotta see this," Eddie exclaimed and pointed to a large carton labeled *The Phantom of the Opera*.

Inside was a craggy-looking rubber mask with bulbous glass eyes, an upturned pig nose, dirt-encrusted, protruding teeth set in a nasty grimace, and a several wires attached to levers.

"What in the world…" she started.

Lon slowly withdrew the different elements and started putting them on. Once the mask was securely in place, he picked up his complicated wiring system and pulled on a couple of the levers.

The result was terrifying. With the phony skin and nose of his mask yanked backward, Lon had created an odd delusion. He no longer seemed human. He had become a monstrous looking creature.

"Oh, my lord," Rosie muttered.

Eddie came behind her and circled his arms around her. "I know, I know. But as scary as it is, it's also amazing, isn't it?"

She gulped.

Later, when the Chaneys hugged her goodnight, she thanked them for a "grand time," and smiled. In the car returning home as Eddie bubbled over about the evening and how happy he was that she finally got to meet the man who had become like a second father to him, she again smiled politely. When he gave her a fast peck on the cheek after they both saw Beatrice spying on them from the archway, she stroked his arm and muttered a "good night".

Once inside, she nodded as she walked past Beatrice to her room, claiming she was "exhausted, but had a lovely night."

She figured Eddie was probably disappointed she hadn't been more exuberant in the car, but she couldn't help it. That terrible mask was still inside her head. Thinking about it now in her bedroom, though, she realized she was grateful for the night at the Chaney's. But she had another priority: her soft, comfy bed. As soon as her head hit the pillow, she was out like a light.

Her recurring dream came back with a vengeance.

Her five-year-old hand crushed into a fist, the little girl pounds on the gray door with the rusty bronze knob. Behind her, sirens are wailing, in front of her, silence, no response from within.

"Anybody there?" the little girl calls out.

No answer, only the sirens growing louder, more piercing.

Now, behind her comes the swirl of flashing lights, spotting the door in front of her with snowdrops of white. The girl turns around. "Leave me alone!" she screams at a faceless man coming toward her.

"But I'm here to help you," he replies. Then he disappears.

The little girl spins around toward the door and knocks again. This time, the door opens a crack.

"A-hah!" the little girl cries out with delight.

But after several seconds, the door is opened as it first was—hardly at all. Frustration makes the child strong. With all her might, she pushes the heavy door and steps inside, where it is dark save for a single ray of light escaping from the next room. An eerie sound penetrates the air, unlike anything she has ever heard. Step-by-step, tip-toe by tip-toe, the girl steps through the darkness into the semi-lit room. There, surrounded by shadows, a man is sitting on a chair, his back to her. A standing lamp is next to him, shining down a hazy glow all around him.

"Who are you? Can you help me?" asks the girl with a quaver.

She can hear the person stir, and when he rises, she sees he is covered with a headscarf.

"Are you the one who's here to help me?" she whispers as he removes the cloth.

Excited to see who her savior is, she steps toward him as he slowly turns around.

But he is not a man. He is Lon Chaney's hideous creature from The Phantom of The Opera.

Rosie jerked to a sitting position, her nightgown soaked in sweat, her heartbeat rattling in her chest. *Is this an omen of bad things to come?*

CHAPTER EIGHT

"There is no other occupation in the world that so closely resembled enslavement as the career of a film star."
— Louise Brooks, actress

January 11, 1926
Seven Days AFTER the Harris Shooting
After Dinner at Lon Chaney's

AS SOON AS Mabel saw Eddie come in from his evening at Lon's, she was surprised to see a slightly long face. Knowing how excited he had been to introduce his girl to the Chaneys, she motioned for him to follow her.

"Come into the parlor for a nightcap." She held up the "special" bottle of port a bootlegger had recently sold to her.

He nodded and stepped into her favorite room in her house. Warm, welcoming, and stuffed to the rafters with memorabilia from her past, she knew it was often a comfort for her boarders to sit in one of her large, high-backed chairs by the fireplace and chat.

After two double shot glasses of the smooth, mellow spirit, he admitted he was frustrated with Rosie, never mind her more-than-hostile mother. Sometimes, he didn't know how to proceed with her.

The old maven clucked maternally, leaned over and patted his knee. "Eddie, I just gotta get this off my chest." She paused. "Why are you so worried about how to behave around Rosie, honey? To me, you've been the very model of patience with her, as she waffles this way or that. Tell me. I'm a good listener, you know."

"I know, Mabel, I know. It's a long story."

She smiled. "Honey, I've got no where's else to go right now, so out with it."

After a long sigh, he started in. He told her how, by the time he was seventeen, he realized girls really seemed to like him. He also could tell fellow boy classmates, and even a few male teachers, envied him. His mother told him he should concentrate on school and helping his dad. His father, however, remained proud of his offspring. As his parents sat on their rockers and watched the evening parade of giggling girls mosey past their front porch asking for their son, Eddie would sit inside and hear his father sometimes joke to his mother, "He got his good looks from me, you know. That's why the girls flock to him."

He paused.

"Go on, honey," Mabel encouraged.

Continuing, Eddie talked about how, as a young, virile man, he enjoyed sexually experimenting with any female he fancied. It seemed these girls—along with numerous mature women—came at him everywhere he went, both day and night. At his father's auto mechanic garage, the local library, the grocery store. Still, he remained uneasy. Instinctively, he knew making use of this kind of potency even with females who were more than willing, was superficial at best. At worst, a pathway to emotional carelessness.

He became so aware of that possibility, he once mentioned his worry to a close friend.

"Are you joking?" His pal laughed. "Grab it while you can, Eddie!" Far from helping him, his friend's advice made him feel even worse.

Sure enough, two years later, his fears came true. Margaret Luther—Maggie, for short—came into his life as a pretty, innocent girl of seventeen. Being shy, she had never actively pursued him, and because of that, he was drawn to her all the more.

They enjoyed bicycle riding out near the hills and crop fields of Fillmore whenever they had a chance. He found that with this relationship, however, there were more limitations than usual. She was from a strict Lutheran family, so she had to be home by ten. She had to go with her family to church every Sunday, and most importantly, by being a "good, proper girl," she was not, under any circumstances, to have sexual relations until marriage.

At first, that last part almost pleased Eddie. Here was his chance to prove he had a deeper conscience than ever before. But all his good intentions soon eroded. After all, he was a normal young man, with normal needs, and what was the real harm to stray a bit from Maggie here or there? He did care for her, but he decided a little care of himself was also important.

He could feel himself slowly detaching from her, and although some guilt crept in, he couldn't help himself. He ignored Maggie's worried looks and blithely continued to cat around—until she finally confronted him.

"Don't you want to be with me anymore, Eddie?" she asked one Saturday afternoon, as they sat under a huge elm tree on her family's property.

Startled, a comeback answer didn't occur to him until it was too late. She turned to him, her tears on the tip of overflowing. "I know you've been seeing other girls, Eddie. I guess I'm not good enough for you?"

He remembered how he had hung his head. "Of course, you are."

Suddenly, Eddie paused his story, his face turning rosy.

"Come on, you gotta tell me what happened next, for goodness sake, Eddie," Mabel said.

Gulping, he told her how Maggie had then leaned in, slowly unbuttoned her blouse, and asked him to make love to her.

"This is just like a dime novel!" Mabel exclaimed.

A single nod, and Eddie finished his story. Apparently, her brother had seen them and told Maggie's parents. Immediately, she was dispatched to an all-girl's school up in Sacramento. Not particularly surprised, Eddie did wish her well. In his own way, he had cared for her. Yet over the years, he regretted how he hadn't tried to contact her. Not even once.

"Still think I'm such a honey?" he asked softly.

"Oh, Eddie," Mabel said. "You were being just a red-blooded American male, is all. For the love of God, get over it."

January 13, 1926
Nine Days AFTER the Harris Shooting
The Following Friday Night

When the wine-red Chrysler Model B-70 with the black top pulled up in front of the Highland Courts, it seemed out of place. Surrounded on the street by mostly low-end Tin Lizzies, its elegant finish and sleek lines immediately garnered attention. People strolled by and stopped, Beatrice hurried outside to the sidewalk to gawk, and everyone present ogled the luxury car with fascination and awe.

As soon as the driver's door opened, a uniformed chauffeur stepped out. With his black jacket and double brass buttons, his matching black and gold-trimmed cap, along with his Jodhpur black pants and black boots, he sported an officious air as he marched up to the apartment complex's main archway and stopped in front of the open-mouthed Beatrice.

"Good evening, Madam. Are you the mother of Miss Rosie Paige?" he asked. "If so, I believe your daughter is expected to accompany Mr. Berns tonight."

After a quick nod, Beatrice almost pushed him aside so she could see into the car's interior. "Is Mr. Berns in the back seat?" She craned her neck. "Please, I would be happy to offer him some tea. Or coffee, perhaps?" She giggled like a schoolgirl.

The chauffeur stared down at her haughtily. "Mr. Berns never comes to the door, much less inside, Madam. He prefers to wait in the car."

"Of course, of course," Beatrice said.

He cleared his throat. "Your daughter is ready to come with me?" His tone resembled a command.

Nodding vigorously, Beatrice scurried inside.

"He's here! He's here!" she gushed to her daughter and Walt sitting on the living room couch, Patches and Ginger wedged between them. "You two should see his car. It's magnificent! And his chauffeur is outside, waiting for our girl right now."

She motioned to Rosie. "Stand up and let me see that dress you borrowed. I want to make sure you're perfect. Get rid of the dog and cat, for goodness sake, and stand up, stand up!"

The shrillness of her mother's voice brought back memories of a time Rosie would rather forget. *Oh, Mama, get a hold of yourself!*

Still, she stood up and performed an exaggerated twirl in front of them.

The "robe de style" dress was black satin, sleeveless, and scoop-necked. Added to the skirt was an overlay of black chiffon with a scalloped hem, edged in gold. Nude-colored stockings, newly polished black shoes, and her standby fake pearls with equally fake earrings all completed the picture.

Walt grinned. "You look very nice."

Beatrice stood back, arms crossed, and eyed her daughter from head to toe. "Well, well, well. You sure look beautiful. I've never been prouder."

Rosie sighed. *Would my mother ever realize just how belittling a remark like that was? How about my brain? My humor? My "gumption," as Clara Bow would say?*

"Well, we mustn't keep Mr. Berns waiting. Here's your wrap, dear." Beatrice handed over one of her own stoles.

As Rosie made her way to the expensive car with the chauffeur, she feared her mother would come out and wave good-bye to her and the producer. But to her relief, Beatrice remained in the apartment. Probably Walt's doing, she figured, as the chauffeur opened one of the back doors for her, his movements practiced, his face deadpan.

"Welcome, my dear," Berns said with an extended hand as she entered the back seat. "Ready for the Brown Derby?"

"Yes, indeed. Looking forward to it." It crossed her mind that her mother should be the one in the car, not her. *Wouldn't Mama just love all of this.*

Passing through Beverly Hills, even in the dark, she couldn't help but notice the discrepancy between the few grand houses lit up with glitzy lights and her own neighborhood, with its small bungalows and modest homes sunk into the shadows.

She could feel his eyes on her in the car as she looked out through the window.

"Cat got your tongue, Miss Paige?" he asked quietly.

"Just taking it all in. It's not every day a girl gets to ride in style like this."

Even his laugh sounded sophisticated—light, sonorous, as if he were at a high-end dinner party filled with educated guests. "You see? You could very well make it in Hollywood. You've got a certain amount of, shall we say, spunk." He turned serious. "Just make sure to use it properly."

What did that last part mean? They pulled up in front of the brand-new restaurant, and the chauffeur stepped around to the curbside car door to let them out.

There stood the Brown Derby, its unique construction a perfect match for a man's derby hat. Brown, bulbous, it made her chuckle.

"Here we are." Berns took her arm and led her through the canopied entrance.

Its inside was as fascinating as its outside façade. A series of delicate, intertwined chandeliers hung from the dome ceiling, creating a tapestry of small, sparkling lights attached to curved holding rods. All the booth seats were made of maroon-colored leather, each table perfect in its service presentation, and the walls were covered not with paintings, but with photograph after photograph of actors and actresses.

As they were guided over plush carpeting to a cozy corner booth toward the back of the room, she wondered why he kept saying to the *maître d'*, "This is perfect, this is perfect."

Once settled into their cushy seats, Berns quickly explained. "My dear, this is a perfect table for viewing. From here, we can easily see whoever comes in."

It was true. No sooner had they been handed two large menus the size of small billboards, she peeked out around hers and noticed Douglas Fairbanks and his wife Mary Pickford, curls and all, strolling up the aisle toward them. Immediately, Rosie let out an involuntary breath as the famous couple both slid into a nearby booth at the last minute.

"Oh, my," she said. "My mother calls them 'royalty.'"

Berns put down his menu with the crack of a smile. No, not really a smile. More of a smirk. She suddenly felt like Alice in Wonderland, stuck in an uncertain world after a perilous trip down the rabbit hole.

"Yes, well, if you follow my lead, Miss Paige, you'll be used to seeing the likes of those two stars. Shall I introduce you to them on our way out?"

She gulped. "I suppose so."

That made him chuckle. "Suppose? Not the response I am used to getting when such an offer is given. But it'll have to do."

He examined the menu for a while, then looked up. "Why don't I just order for the both of us, hmm?"

She started to protest with a polite "No, thanks," but he wasn't listening. He signaled a waiter over and proceeded to order two steaks—bloody rare––scalloped potatoes, and creamed spinach.

"I was thinking about having their Cobb salad," she muttered as the waiter took her menu away. Walt had recently regaled her with stories about how since the Cobb family basically owned this unique, new restaurant, they were offering a special salad, named after them.

Berns was already moving on. "Now, tell me about your past experience. Were you in burlesque? Modeling?" he quizzed.

"No." She shook her head. "None of that. This is it. No before. Just the present."

Eyes slit in observation mode, he leaned back and studied her closely, as if appraising a new suit. "You're good with the comeback lines. Have you ever thought of doing comedy?"

"Oh no, no," she said with a little snort.

"Don't say no until you've tried it. Look at Mabel Normand. She's quite attractive and funny, to boot."

Images of Mabel Normand in *The Extra Girl*, with her rolled eyes and her comic feigning of a femme fatale came to mind. *Didn't Mama and I just laugh and laugh that day in the theater!* Her mind then spun its way into her mother's warning about Mabel's drug habits.

"And what about Marion Davies?" he continued. "Now that's a beautiful young lady with such an expressive face!"

"But isn't she controlled by William Randall Hearst these days?"

He stiffened. "So?"

"Just commenting, is all." She shrugged. Maybe Eddie was right. Producers, newspaper magnets, and politicians tend to stick together.

But all thoughts of politics disappeared when their steaks arrived, and Rosie tried hard not to gag. Bloody rare? How about not cooked at all, except to maybe drag the meat across a grill for two seconds each.

"Bon appetite," the producer said, digging into his with more relish than she would imagine such a fancy man would do. She fiddled with her potatoes and spinach.

After he finished, he settled back against the leather. "Now, this is what I want you to do. Get a resumé going, whether it's true or not, and also, a full wardrobe."

"What kind of clothes are we talking about on my salary?" On top of still feeling a little hungry, she could feel herself becoming annoyed

He looked her up and down. "More dresses like what you're wearing tonight. Very nice, my dear."

He suddenly leaned over, and with a pincer grasp, picked up something off her shoulder strap then held it up into the light. It was one of Patches' long hairs.

"Dog hair? Cat hair?" he asked. His sneer was obvious.

He began talking about the merits of the different moguls and producers, how in this business, catching their attention was the only way to climb up the food chain. His discourse remained fluid, endless, until he suddenly stopped.

"Ah," he muttered, jiggling his hand in the air in a little wave. "There's Charlie Chaplin with someone I don't recognize. And there's—" he hesitated.

Curious, she glanced up and over toward the nearby table where his eyes seemed to be focused. There was nothing unusual there, just an unattractive, heavy-set middle-aged man, bulging out of his suit with a young woman, all dressed up. The man glanced at her briefly, then nodded at Berns.

Berns didn't nod back. He just carried on, this time discussing Charlie Chaplin's mansion, and all the great parties he had attended there.

Mama should definitely be the one here, not me. She grew more disinterested by the minute.

Oblivious to her silence, Berns stopped once again, this time about dessert.

"I hear they have fabulous desserts here."

"Oh? That'll be fun," she said, excited for the first time since they had sat down.

The waiter came over with a dessert cart. On it were six sweet concoctions that made Rosie's mouth water. He started his monologue. "Tonight, we have Pineapple and Raspberry Neapolitan, a Berry short-cake, Strawberry Puffs, chocolate hearts, and a customer favorite, our Dessert Cocktail." He stood back, took out his pad and pencil, and asked politely, "Now, what will you have, Miss?"

She clasped her hands together with a tiny cupping sound.

"I'll have the Neapolitan, please."

"Excellent choice. And for you, sir?"

"Just coffee. Watching my waistline." Berns patted his stomach.

The waiter nodded and with a smooth about-turn, disappeared.

No sooner had he left, Berns turned to her. "Do think about these kinds of desserts, Miss Paige. It would serve you well to watch your waistline, too. I've known many a starlet who didn't take care of herself. Not good, not good, my dear."

Rosie stared at him. *Then why, in heaven's name, did you bring up their great desserts?*

He droned on, this time imparting his various theories about Hollywood. How it was he alone who managed this or that, how if it weren't for him, various stars would have gone nowhere.

In no time at all, she had stopped listening, choosing to play the same trick she sometimes used with Beatrice to make her mother think she was paying attention when she really wasn't. As the movie producer continued on, she stared at a spot on his forehead, an inch or two over his eyes, and just like it did with her mother, her ploy seemed to be working. Judging by his smug face, he obviously thought she was giving him her utmost attention. By the time his coffee arrived with her delicious looking dessert, she had lost her appetite.

Fifteen minutes later, Berns glanced over at her one-third eaten Neapolitan, tossed out a Cheshire cat grin, and took out his pocket watch.

"Look at the time. Well, my dear, I'm afraid the evening's going to have to end. I have a big meeting with the studio heads in the morning."

"Oh?"

His eyes looked more intense. "Yes, how to handle this Chester Harris case. Everyone's quite nervous about it." He paused. "But you didn't hear that from me."

Not that again, she thought. If nothing else tonight, it had been good to get away from all the news consumption by Beatrice and Walt these days. Also, it was a breath of fresh air not to think about the murderer who was still at large.

He stood up and plunked down several large bills onto the table. Obviously, her cue to rise and leave with him. Now.

They didn't get far. Several steps up their aisle they were stopped by America's golden couple, Douglas Fairbanks and Mary Pickford.

"Berns, old chap, how are you this fine evening?" Douglas asked.

Rosie could tell he had been drinking without even looking at the three empty wine bottles on the table. His words slurred together.

Mary Pickford wasn't so cordial. "Who's your latest filly, Berns? Hmm?" The actress' big doe eyes, known worldwide for their soft kindness, were now aimed at Rosie. They were cold and piercing.

Rosie met her gaze head on. Her mother's story about the star's curls coming from prostitutes suddenly loomed large. She bit her lip and resisted giggling.

"May I introduce you both to Rosie Paige. Rosie, as you can see, this is

Mary Pickford and Douglas Fairbanks.

Douglas stood up, gallantly bowed, then took the bit player's hand and kissed it. "Pleased to meet you, Miss Paige. I assume you are an actress?"

"Don't be a horse's behind, Doug," Mary hissed.

Ignoring "America's sweetheart," Rosie nodded politely and opened her mouth to reply, but Berns answered for her. "Yes, she is. As a matter of fact, we were just discussing her career at dinner, Douglas."

Mary looked her up and down. "I'll bet. Good luck on that one." Her voice sounded bitter.

Rosie didn't miss a beat. "Thank you, Miss Pickford. By the way, I've always admired your luscious curls." She resisted a titter. "I was thinking of buying extra curls for myself and wondered if you might possibly know where I could purchase any?"

She almost felt sorry for the celebrity. Pickford's eyes widened in shock; her face showed a flush. On the other hand, Fairbank's expression seemed to be an inscrutable mix of emotions.

Berns grabbed her elbow and said, "Nice to see you two. Enjoy your meal."

As he guided her out to the car, his grip on her arm felt like a handcuff. *Me and my overactive tongue. He's probably gonna drop me. And won't Mama be furious.*

But to her surprise, in the limo he oozed charm and graciousness. "Well, my dear, I must say, this evening has been an eye-opener for me."

"Mr. Berns, look, I'm sorry if I was rude to Miss Pickford," she said. "I can be too outspoken at times."

Hearing his chuckle was a completely relief. "It probably did that woman some good," he said. "She's definitely not how the public sees her."

"Oh?" *Is he going to tell me the story about the prostitutes? Finally, an interesting topic.*

"Tough as nails, she is."

And?

That was all he offered on the subject. "No, it's all right, my dear. In fact, I believe you passed the test."

She could feel her body tense. "What test?" Eddie's warnings were beginning to reverberate in her head.

"How you will be able to hold your own at a party at Gloria Swanson's in two weeks."

"What?" *Mama definitely should be here!*

"Yes, I feel that will be a good avenue in which to introduce you to people, who—well, frankly—matter."

A party at Clara Bow's, and now this? It was all happening so fast. Too fast. Images of her gleeful mother, faithful Walt, and cautious Eddie swirled around in her brain as the car travelled east on Wilshire Boulevard. In the distance she could hear the clang of a trolley car, the toots of a few automobile horns, and unnerving howls from a pack of coyotes up in the hills that separated Los Angeles from the San Fernando Valley.

As they turned north on Cahuenga Boulevard into Hollywood, the lull in conversation gave her a chance to think about Clara Bow and her declaration that, "Hollywood society doesn't accept me." All of a sudden, she felt an urge to ask Berns the same question she had asked the friendly, but shunned actress.

"Can I bring my boyfriend as a date?" She smiled, thinking of Clara's warm reaction to that very same question.

In the backseat, the silence stretched long and thick. "Ah, no, Miss Paige," he said finally. "That would not be advisable. After all, if I'm to introduce you to the right people, that wouldn't be good. Besides, he would just be bored."

"I suppose."

He shook his head. "There you go, supposing again, Rosie. May I call you Rosie?"

Nodding, she felt a slight tightness in her chest. Then she chided herself. He had been a perfect gentleman all evening. Not a hint of a big time "cuddler" so many of the girls complained about—the men who liked to get some real petting action, in exchange for helping them.

"Rosie, if I'm going to assist you in obtaining a successful career, you must trust me. It's not just that I've been around the block, you know. I'm successful because I know what works in this town, and what doesn't. So just relax and let me guide you through the ropes, all right?"

She was about to nod when, to her dismay, they had reached her home. There was Beatrice outside, waving enthusiastically. Walt was weaving back and forth as he, too, attempted to wave. Was he actually drunk? It was a good thing Mr. Berns couldn't see her face. It would have displayed her complete mortification.

The producer seemed unfazed by it all. "Interesting neighborhood you have here," he muttered. Then, when the chauffeur opened up her side to help her out, he called out, "Get some beauty sleep. Now off you go." He made a little hand gesture, as if shooing away a fly.

Left on the curb by the chauffeur, she heard the directive, "Drive on home. Now!" from the backseat as Beatrice and an unsteady Walt surrounded her.

"Good night, Rosie-Posey," he slurred, his Brownie camera tucked under his arm. "I'll catch up with you both tomorrow and get tonight's big scoop."

She knew Beatrice would be extremely disappointed, but as soon as they both went inside, she announced, "Mama, I'm just exhausted. All I want to do is get some sleep. Let's talk tomorrow at breakfast, all right?"

She was right. Beatrice's face fell, and fell hard. She hugged her mother goodnight and made it to her bedroom, alone, where she instantly collapsed, without even shedding her clothes. Yet even with her eyes closed and her body feeling like dead weight, one thing popped into her head, seconds before she crashed. It was Douglas Fairbank's face, clear as a bell, with his mixed expression when he had looked at her. There had been a little bit of admiration at her "spunk," but a much heftier dose of pity and concern.

CHAPTER NINE

"Let's keep that our little secret, shall we?"
— Aimee Semple McPherson, famous Evangelist

January 14, 1926
Ten Days AFTER the Harris Shooting
The Morning after Rosie's Dinner with Berns

"SO, TELL ME, tell me!" Beatrice demanded, a half-filled coffee cup clutched tightly in her hand.

Barely out of her bedroom, Rosie blinked twice and yawned. "Can I at least go to the bathroom first, Mama?"

Beatrice scowled. "Of course, but hurry. I've been waiting for over an hour for you to get up. Come into the kitchen when you're finished. Walt's already here."

He managed to make it over so early? The image of a wobbly Walt from the night before was still fresh in her mind.

In the kitchen, she immediately detected a whiff of gin. There he was, huddled over a cup of coffee. In front of him lay the *Los Angeles Times*, strewn across the kitchen table, with its new headline: "Chester Harris Memorial Today. Killer Still At Large."

"Really?" Rosie sighed as she poured herself a big cup of coffee. "Can't we please have a break from this case? I know you love murder mysteries,

Walt, but I think the police are handling it. Have a little faith. Remember, I was there that day. I sure don't need to be reminded of it all the time."

"Rosie. Be nice. Just because you never read the newspapers, doesn't mean Walt and I don't get to." Beatrice picked up the newspaper, folded it in half, and placing it aside, looked at him. "Sorry, Walt," she said gently.

Patches trotted over, wagging his tail furiously, then leapt up onto Rosie's lap.

"Hey there, boy," she cooed and gave him a little kiss on the top of his head. "I'll take you for a walk as soon as I finish my coffee." She gently placed him down beside her.

Beatrice's palm hit the table with a loud smack. "Enough stalling, Rosie!"

"All right, Mama, all right." The actress looked at both of them sitting across from her and shrugged. "Basically, Mr. Berns feels I could become an actress of note." She let Patches lick her nose.

"I knew it!" Beatrice exclaimed, beaming. She turned to Walt seated next to her. "Didn't I say that, Walt?"

He produced a crooked grin. "You sure did, Bea. Looks like our girl's gonna make it to the top. Let me take a picture of her."

"Oh, Walt," Rosie said, annoyed, as he flashed a quick one of her with her mouth still open. "Nice one, Walt. Thank you."

"Details, please," Beatrice placed her elbows on the table.

"He told me to create a resumé and get more clothes. Dresses like what I wore last night."

Her mother's eyes darted around the kitchen. "Oh? Just like that, with no offer to pay for them himself? I don't know if we can afford…"

"I immediately mentioned my small salary, Mama."

"And what did he say?"

"Not much. He was too busy talking about how he would help me meet the right people, how he knew the Hollywood business. You know, a real sales pitch."

"Aw, heck, Bea," Walt broke in, swatting his hand up into the air. "Don't worry. I got some cash stashed away. It's yours for the taking."

"I can't let you do that," Beatrice said. "You've done so much for us already."

"Anything for you two."

Rosie shook her head. All of a sudden, he appeared so haggard to her. *When did that happen?* Ginger suddenly jumped up onto her lap. Immediately, the cat started purring so loudly, they all paused to stare at her.

Beatrice snorted. "Enough with these pets, Rosie! I can't move around here without one of them always being underfoot. Maybe if you concentrated more on Hollywood and less on your obsession about stray animals, you'd get somewhere."

"Where, pray tell, would I 'get?'" She stroked her cat's back, and the purrs grew even louder.

"I blame your father," Beatrice said angrily.

Rosie steeled herself. *Here we go again.*

"As soon as he left, you insisted on bringing home all these mangy, flea-bitten animals off the street. You…"

Walt put his hand on her arm and gave it a slight pat. "Bea," he muttered. "Let's go into the living room, why don't we?" He rose unsteadily.

"Good idea, Walt." Rosie stood up as well. "Coming, Mama?"

Beatrice nodded, her lips tight.

In the living room, another newspaper was strewn across the coffee table, its headline even more succinct: "Is Los Angeles Safe with a Killer on the Loose?"

Rosie, grateful for a respite from her mother's tirade, picked up the paper and started reading it silently. Within seconds, Patches had jumped up and flopped down on the sofa between her and Walt.

"Walt, you're right," she said after a minute or two. "This is important news. Almost two weeks later and still no leads."

She continued reading, then looked up. "Still, even if Harris wasn't nice, it must be sad for his family today." She paused. "Don't know why they call it a memorial, though."

"They've already buried him," Beatrice said. "The ladies in the costume room told me Jewish people do that, you know. They bury their loved ones right away. So, when he was put in the ground, it was a service just for the family. This observance today is going to be for everyone else."

"I still think it's a sad thing," Rosie said. "Don't you agree, Walt?"

"Walt?" Beatrice repeated his name softly.

For a moment he didn't answer.

"You okay, Walt?" Rosie asked.

"Sad, you say?" he said thickly. "You have no idea about sad." His face suddenly harbored a pinched brow as tears pooled in his eyes.

"Forget about that damn Harris," he continued. "Try this one on for size.

Try watching your wife and daughter be killed by a trolley car. How about seeing my little girl, Julia, hit so hard, her body flew a good twenty feet before she landed on the ground with a thud?" He swiped both his eyes and continued. "Try seeing your wife, also hit, crawl over to her and the both of them die right before I could reach them. Try…"

Sitting across from him, Beatrice outstretched her hand. "Walt. I'm so sorry."

Barely acknowledging her, he drew a shaky breath as Patches jumped down to the floor and curled around his legs.

"And then there's my son," he continued, still obviously agitated. "He was over in Europe for the Great War." He shook his head. "He used to write me letters all the time. Wrote me once how he and the other men loved seeing Charlie Chaplin films, how it made them forget their miserable lives in those trenches. Those mud holes they were forced to stay in as bombs exploded all around them. Ironic, isn't it? That I ended up leaving the film business, even though Chaplin gave my son great comfort."

"Where's your son living now?" Rosie put her hand on his arm.

The human contact seemed to pull him back from wherever his mind had been.

"He never made it back," he said dully.

Stunned, the two women looked at each other.

"Walt, I don't know what to say," Beatrice said gently. "I just…"

He interrupted her. "Funny, how all you're left with are the odd, little things, 'cause you throw out everything else to ease the pain. Things like the necklace my wife loved that her mother gave her as a child. My daughter's teddy bear I gave her for Christmas one year, almost in shreds now, and as for my son…"

"What?" they chorused.

"His sergeant sent me his ID, his canteen, and a few other things."

For several seconds, they were engulfed by silence. Then Walt suddenly stood up and Patches let loose a startled whimper. Still wobbly, Walt pressed his hand down on a sofa arm to steady himself.

"Gotta go." He avoided their eyes as he reached for his jacket slung over a nearby chair.

Beatrice got up and came over to him. With her arms around his waist, her head rested on his chest. "Oh, Walt," she said, "we're your family now. Don't ever forget that."

"That's right, Walt," Rosie said, nodding.

His eyes finally focused on them. "Thanks, girls. Yes, you're my family now. And Rosie? I guess you're my daughter all grown up."

At the police station, Frank had just made it over to his desk when Captain Billings charged over and grabbed his arm.

"Come into my office. Now," he commanded.

The room was packed that morning, filled with several handcuffed thugs ready to be charged or incarcerated. A drunk already behind bars, in the process of drying out, kept screaming at the top of his lungs, until someone bellowed, "Quit your yowling, or I'll shut you up for good!"

En route to the captain's office, Frank noticed a traffic cop shoving extra cash into his pocket without even bothering to look around. *The balls on these damn traffic guys. They don't even try to hide the dough they're palming on a daily basis.* He sighed. Sometimes keeping clean took too much out of him.

Billings closed his office door with a bang. After shutting his Venetian blinds, he muttered, "Damn."

"Sir?" Frank took a seat as Billings plopped down behind his desk and held up several assorted papers.

"Know what these are, Lozano?"

"I have no idea."

"They're letters from the studio and private citizens demanding we catch the Harris killer." He crunched the papers into a large ball with one hand. "Enough of this pussyfooting around, Lozano. You get me an arrest, or else."

"Or else?"

"Or else we plant some evidence."

Frank gulped. "Sir?"

"Yeah, that guy…" He looked through his notes. "That Willis guy. I want you to put something in his car. Give us a reason to bring him in as the main suspect." He took a rifle shell out of his top drawer. "See? This here is similar to what the killer used in his 1903 Springfield."

"Sir, I don't think…" Frank started.

"I don't give a damn what you think, detective. You do it, or I'll get someone who ain't so high an' mighty to do it for you. Someone who will take action when you won't."

Frank's teeth fused into a tight clench. "What kind of action are we talking about?"

"Any kind of harassment, detective. You name it. Tail him, call him, pound on his door at night. Or do what I just asked you to do."

A knock on the door gave both of them a start.

"Come in," the captain barked.

It was Frank's partner, Shire. "Sorry, sir, but there's a woman named Sheila Morgan here to see you."

Billings groaned. "Harris' step-sister. Again? What does she want this time?"

"Well, sir, she's pretty worked up."

"Of course, she is. She's crazy and doesn't realize when she's not welcome. She's a real mustard plaster, if you ask me." He blew out a puff of air. "Okay, Shire, tell her I'll get to her when I can."

As soon as Shire left, Billings slowly swiveled around toward Frank. "You," he said smugly.

"Sir?" Frank could feel a creeping sensation crawl up the back of his neck.

"Yeah, you, detective. This is your assignment since you aren't so willing to do the other thing I asked of you."

"I don't understand."

"Get this Morgan dame off my back. Listen to her Jesus holy-roller dribble and do whatever she needs. Just don't let her come in here all the time." His intense eyes bore a hole into Frank. "Can you at least manage to do that for me, detective?"

Frank stood up. "Yes, sir, I can," he said, suddenly thinking of more pleasant things, such as numerous stiff drinks. Or passing out on his couch. Or Rosie.

The last time Frank had seen Harris' step-sister, she had definitely appeared to be slightly off-kilter. This time as he approached her, she seemed akin to a vagabond. Besides the dark circles under her eyes, three prominent, maroon-colored food stains had become embedded down the front of her dress, as if days earlier she had eaten spaghetti sauce or ketchup in a hurry. Her jacket had a large rip on its left collar, one stocking had a hole at her knee, and her hat was askew, undoubtedly shoved down at the last minute as an afterthought.

Masking his repugnance, Frank attempted civility. "Hello, Miss Morgan.

My name is Detective Lozano. What can I do for you this morning?"

When she stepped in close, Frank resisted an urge to bat away her strong scent. Backing off a pace, he settled on her expression. It was one of total anguish. Her wide eyes and trembling lips made him think of the phrase, *But for the grace of God.* He softened.

"Let's go to my desk, shall we, Miss Morgan? You can tell me what you need there."

That seemed to pacify her. Not so with him. Escorting her back to his desk, the comments uttered by his colleagues when they passed them by made him cringe.

"Lozano's got himself a new girl."

"Who dragged her in?"

"What a loony bin."

At his desk, he pulled up a chair, motioned her to sit, and opened his mouth to apologize for the male rudeness. But it soon became obvious she was unaware of anything else but her own quest. He kept his mouth shut.

"I wanted to tell Captain Billings about my idea on how to capture Chester's murderer. Is he around?" Her eyes blazed, and her hands twisted into a ball of fingers.

"He's busy, but I can help you, Miss Morgan. What's your idea?"

"Have you heard of 'Sister,' Detective Lozano?"

One eyebrow arched. "Do you mean your sister?"

"No, no, no. The one and only Sister." Her stare intensified. "Aimee Semple McPherson is Sister to all of God's followers," she added.

Oh, brother. He sighed.

"Detective, since the captain is busy, I want you and me to go see her because she is also a prophet, and I believe she might have some answers regarding where the killer is."

Are you kidding me? He tried not to snort. "I don't think—"

Her next words bubbled out in double-time. "Listen, detective, if you won't go with me, I shall have to go to the papers. Your captain isn't listening, you people haven't arrested anyone, and it's time to get some answers."

He put his palms up. "All right, all right," he said. "You want to go now?"

She scoffed. "Of course not, you silly man. Sister only does this at night, after her meetings. Meet me at Angelus Temple at eight-fifteen. Don't be late. It's not good if you're late."

Frank shook his head. *All these years of policing, and it's come down to this?* "All right. I'll meet you out front no later than eight-fifteen."

When she marched out of the room, all thoughts of salvaging his career went with her.

After a day of craziness, by five o'clock, Frank had only one thing on his mind. He figured if he took his time, Rosie might be leaving the Medford lot around then, and there was a strong possibility he'd be able to see her. *Can't believe I'm doing this.* Still, there he was, a few yards down the block from Eddie's car, waiting to catch a glimpse of her.

By late afternoon, various actors and actresses in full costume were slowly trickling out of the front gates. He casually eyed them all. Cowboys strolled by next to ancient gladiators. Saloon gals locked arms with scantily dressed flappers. A circus clown placed his arm around the waist of a pretty ballerina squeezed into her pink tutu.

All of a sudden, Frank jerked his body upright. There was Williams, the rookie detective from out of state, fumbling with Eddie's car lock. Frank saw him glance to the right, then to the left before he entered the automobile. The cop stayed inside the car for less than a minute. Then, with a quiet close of the Tin Lizzy's front door, Williams made a fast getaway.

Damn! Billings got that patsy to do this. He watched Eddie and Rosie slowly approach the Tin Lizzy.

Charging out of the front gates, a thin, well-dressed young man in a dark suit appeared, taking odd, short steps over toward Eddie. Frank snorted. *Henry Blake. What the hell does he want with Eddie?* Taking it all in, he stayed rooted to his seat. But when Blake suddenly turned to Rosie and seized her arm, Frank grabbed his door handle and started to exit the car.

He stopped.

Eddie was already on it. He pulled Rosie behind him protectively and stood chest to chest with the slender man. After a few loud, indistinguishable exchanges, Blake turned around quickly and retreated down the block.

Staring out his windshield, Frank saw Eddie put his arm around Rosie's shoulder, presumably to make sure she was all right. Instantly, the detective pulled out his flask, swilled down several gulps, then watched Eddie open the car on her side. As if by osmosis, before Rosie got in, she slowly rotated around toward the detective, and in spite of what had just happened to her and Eddie, gave a tiny nod to Frank before getting in. *A thank you for thinking I was there, watching over them?* Then he saw Eddie, frozen on the curb, glaring at him. There was certainly no thanks coming from him. A wave of surprise washed over Frank. *Damn, why aren't I more pleased that Eddie probably will be arrested soon?*

Lit up against the dark night sky, the round-edged, multi-columned Temple Angelus positively glowed. Reminiscent of the Roman Coliseum, its simple splendor was a startling contrast to the modest buildings surrounding it.

Once Frank exited his car, he was struck by not only the enormity of the structure, but also the conspicuous black and white signs hanging from its eaves. AIMEE SEMPLE MCPHERSON on one of them. On the other: FOUR SQUARE GOSPEL was displayed immediately below that.

What am I getting myself into? Suddenly, Sheila Morgan grabbed his arm at the front entrance and eagerly pushed him inside. Two steps into the main theater, he noticed multiple filled seats were stacked up in a series of three-tiered balconies. *Probably as much as five thousand seats.* A large choir was singing full force, and masses of people of all colors—Negroes, Latinos, Asians, as well as Caucasians—were in the middle of the floor, stretching out their arms, crying, "Foursquare Gospel says it all!"

"So many different walks of life here," Frank said.

Sheila nodded vehemently and pointed toward a small platform. "Yes, Detective Lozano. Sister feels we're all God's children. There she is!"

Aimee Semple McPherson stood on the stage, dressed in a sparkling white, nurse-like uniform accompanied by a dark cape. Her tight, cropped curls surrounded a very attractive, winning face, and with her arms raised, her head held high, she spoke in an ultra-clear, melodious tone.

"I leave you tonight with only one thought: You have no business being sick! Every one of you should get well and get up and go to work. Earn some money to help send the gospel out. And remember, our Foursquare Gospel: Jesus is our savior. Jesus is the healer. Jesus is the baptizer with the Holy Spirit, and Jesus is—what?"

The entire crowd finished her sentence. "The soon-coming King!" they hollered.

She smiled. "Amen. Good night, and God bless you all!"

"Praise you, Sister!" someone shouted. Instantly, a swell of voices rang out from every corner of the vast, multi-layered auditorium, echoing that sentiment and creating a wall of sound that shook the foundation.

Damn. She may be crazy as a loon, but she sure knows how to pack 'em in. The studios should get a hold of her. They really should.

With the chorus singers now clapping in rhythm and the people slowly exiting, Sheila clutched his arm.

"Look at Sister. She's nodding at me."

"Oh, for goodness sake. She..." He paused. *Helluva thing.* McPherson *was* looking at Sheila. And nodding regally, as if she were Queen Mary of England.

"She told me to wait until everyone's gone. Then we can meet with her in her private office."

Truly curious now, Frank almost looked forward to being up close to this obvious celebrity he had known nothing about before. But it was not to be. When he and Sheila advanced toward Sister, she held up one hand.

"Wait a minute, Sheila. You told me this was just for you. I don't want any stranger in this session. It's highly personal." Her cautious words were in direct contrast to the welcoming warmth she had displayed a mere quarter hour before.

"But this is a detective involved in my step-brother's case."

"Yes, Miss McPherson. I am trying to help Miss Morgan," Frank said. *Even though it's probably a waste of time.*

The evangelist drew herself up an inch taller. "No, this is a *very* personal thing."

"But—" Sheila said.

"If you want a reading," McPherson said, "then it has to be just the two of us. Or, if you like, I can ask someone from the ministry to join us, but not—"

"Detective Lozano," Frank provided.

"I'm sorry," Sister said.

"All right," Sheila replied meekly and muttered to Frank, "Sorry. I was hoping for a lift home."

He shrugged. "Don't worry. Go, do whatever you have to do. I'll wait here for you."

He ended up sitting on a pew, perusing one of Sister's magazines, *Foursquare*, and coming to a realization. She did have a spark all right, and she was doing some good for the needy. But in the end, she was just a self-important, holy-roller and craved the spotlight, just like the biggest of Hollywood's movie stars.

When Sheila returned alone, her face flushed, her eyes bright, Frank asked, "So?"

"I'll tell you in the car. It may be very important," she said.

In the car, he asked her point blank, "So what did McPherson say?"

"Sister said it's wonderful to be alive if Jesus is in your heart…"

"Yeah, yeah, but what did she say regarding your step-brother?"

When Sheila finally told him, he shook his head. Talk about a wild goose chase! He dropped her off at her apartment then returned to his, immediately downing multiple shots of gin. Within minutes, as he bent down to pick up the phone to make a call, he tripped on its cord and was almost catapulted across the room. Sprawled on the floor, he reached for the phone and pulled it toward him. W*hat a waste of time.*

Eddie's day had been long and frustrating as well. Assigned to a new set without Lon Chaney, he found it both boring and irritating. Rosie wasn't there either, and he realized just how much he missed catching her eye and doing their special signal. He missed seeing what she was wearing for her different roles, whether it be a flapper, a party guest, or a dowdy young housewife. But most of all, he missed meeting her afterward to connect and hopefully do some kissing and petting.

Exhausted, he was drifting off to a much-needed sleep when the knock on his door startled him fully awake.

"Eddie, it's me, Mabel," came his landlady's voice.

With a two-legged swing out of bed, he shuffled over to his door. There she was, wrapped in a twenty-year-old bathrobe, a mass of curlers on her head, cold cream slathered over her face and neck. He couldn't help but chuckle.

"I know, I know. I ain't the prettiest sight right now," she said, "but I'm not here for some loving! There's a phone call for you."

He looked over at his clock. "Really? At eleven p.m.?"

"That's what I said when it rang," she muttered and walked with him down the hall to the wall phone. "It ain't your girl, by the way. I know *her* voice."

He picked up the dangling receiver. "Hello?"

The silence on the other end lasted only a couple of seconds. Then came a click.

"Again?" Mabel asked.

Eddie nodded. "What did the person sound like on the other end this time?"

"It was a man, all right," she said, "but he just sounded odd, is all, and his words were—"

"Yeah?"

"Just like the other time, his words were muffled, like he had a hand over his mouth."

"Who did this guy ask for?"

"Willis. No mister, just Willis."

"After what happened to me and Rosie outside of Medford, it's probably Henry Blake, Harris' aide. You know, the one I told you about. He's crazy enough to do something like this." He paused. "But then again, it could also be Pete Roberts, a cameraman. He's made it clear how much he likes Rosie. I've also seen him so stinking drunk on the set a few times, the camera's tripod almost toppled over." He paused a second time. "Or it could be that damn Detective Lozano, just making my life miserable. Take your pick."

CHAPTER TEN

"Your naked body should only belong to those who fall in love with your naked soul."
— Charlie Chaplin, actor

January 21, 1926
Two and a Half Weeks AFTER the Harris Murder

CLARA BOW'S PARTY, set at the unfashionable five o'clock hour, had Beatrice scoffing. Why in the world would such a big star set up an event like that so early? she asked her daughter. Didn't she realize how guileless that was? How, according to the studio costumers, it was just not the thing most celebrities would do?

Rosie shook her head. Where was all that Hollywood-make-it-to-the-top encouragement? Didn't her mama realize what a big box office draw Clara had become? She stood back and defiantly took an exaggerated pose in her party outfit. The knee-high, delicately floral printed shift had only one ornament—a large matching bow attached at her hipline. With her bell-like Clouche hat, Mary Jane shoes, and small, Bakelite earrings, she was the perfect picture of casual wear.

Her sassy posture worked. Beatrice glowered at the ensemble. "No elegance," she said.

"Clara told me personally she not only wanted me to dress casually,"

Rosie said, "she wanted to make the party early enough for her football player friends to have a quick game on her front lawn before the real celebrating began, Mother." Each syllable of "Mother" was uttered with exaggerated distain.

"Hmm," Beatrice muttered.

Rosie held back a smirk. Unlike when she was a child, she now knew how to get to her mother. She watched Beatrice close her mouth with a tiny plop.

The double rap on their door could only mean one thing. It was Eddie. Walt had a key, and the specific rhythm of the knock was something the carpenter and Rosie had rehearsed for each secret Medford Studios' rendezvous. Ignoring her mother's sour face, she hurried to open up to him.

There he was, looking so handsome, so sturdy. Or, as Clara had called him, the Big Six—a big, strong man. His shirt and tie were covered not by a suit jacket, but a V-necked, checkerboard sweater, tastefully fitted, yet still tight enough to show off his muscular arms and chest underneath. His pants were khaki-colored jodhpurs, and instead of shoes, he was wearing tall, dark brown leather boots.

"Wow," Rosie said, her eyes bright. This was pure Eddie. And obviously why he always had a trail of female looks lingering after him wherever he went.

"Wow, is right," he said, eyeing her up and down in her own outfit. Then his gaze slowly traveled down toward his right leg. Her dog Patches was furiously trying to hump it. "I guess Patches approves of me, too," he said, laughing.

Beatrice huffed. Without looking at their visitor, she snapped, "Rosie, get that damn dog off him."

"Come on, boy, let it go, let it go." Rosie pulled Patches off Eddie, and shooed the tail-wagging canine off into the hallway.

Eddie adjusted his tie. "It's not that big a deal, Mrs. Paige."

For a couple of seconds, Beatrice didn't respond. Then, with her arms folded, her legs firmly cemented to the floor, she looked him straight in the eye. "Not too late tonight, you hear me?" she said in a clipped tone.

Oh, Mama. Rosie looked over at Eddie, to see his reaction.

He just nodded. "Yes, ma'am."

"Your mama sure does love me," Eddie commented dryly as they drove away.

Lost in her thoughts, Rosie said nothing.

"Something on your mind?" he asked. He glanced at her, then back to the road.

"Where *were* you last night?" she blurted out. "I thought we had a date."

This time he kept his eyes on the road. "Thought I told you. Something came up for Lon is all."

"No, you didn't." Visions of how she had waited by the phone the night before, battling thoughts of him going out with another girl and fearing he would end up like her father, had been ugly reminders of things she had sworn to herself she would never, ever think about again.

"Look, Rosie, I'm sorry. It was something I had to do. It couldn't be helped," he said. When the light turned red, he stopped the car and turned to face her. "Please don't turn it into something bigger. You've got to trust me a little."

"All right," she said softly. As silence overtook them, she pressed her red lips into a thin line, making their color all but disappear.

"Rosie, please believe me. I was..."

"Another man shot! Another man shot!" a newsboy nearby suddenly yelled.

"What?" Rosie whispered. She opened her car door. "What are you saying?" she cried out to the boy.

The light turned green, and Eddie put a hand on her shoulder. "Rosie, Rosie, close the door! We gotta go."

"But I need to find out about this."

"Later, we'll find out later. For now, let's go to Clara's," he said. "Frankly, what with that detective and Harris' crazy aide, Blake, coming after us, I've had my fill of violence."

She closed her door, he revved up the engine, and they continued on toward Beverly Hills, passing blocks of white bungalow houses and apartments, then several stately homes before she spoke.

"Scary, isn't it?" she said. "I wonder if it's the same person who killed Harris. What do you think?" Her voice held a small tremor.

Eddie kept on driving.

"Eddie?"

He half turned toward her for a couple of seconds. "What?"

"Do you think the new shooting was done by the same Harris killer?"

He shrugged. "Who knows?" He pulled up in front of Clara's mansion. "We're here."

As soon as they got out of the car, they stood side by side, gaping at the scene before them. A large, manicured lawn appeared to be home to a group of thick-muscled, sweaty young men in leather helmets. Barreling toward each other, the football players ran, blocked, tackled, and threw long passes the length of the front yard until someone from the sidelines called out, "Time out!"

Instantly, their manly grunts intermingled with howls of laughter. Five beautiful women began circulating all around them to hand out whisky and gin. No shot glasses, Rosie noticed, but full bottles, one for each player.

By the time she and Eddie walked up the front path, all the players were sitting cross-legged across the grass, guzzling alcohol as fast as they could.

"Welcome to Clara's." Eddie shook his head.

Rosie's tone was cool. "Clara's a free spirit, is all. Nothing wrong in that." She strode toward the front entrance.

Catching up with her, Eddie took her hand as they both stepped inside.

Rosie's first thought was this must be what it was like to be in a speakeasy. Live Charleston music blared with such force, Eddie's effort to talk to her looked like he was just mouthing his words. When she tried to move but couldn't, Eddie leaned over and shouted in her ear.

"This is crazy," he yelled. "Come with me."

Gripping her hand tighter, he used one muscular shoulder and arm to ram their way through the cackling crowd until finally, they reached a side room that was much less inhabited. They both drew deep breaths.

"Boy, that was something," he said, then paused. "Rosie, about last night, I know that may have been hard for you, but I just couldn't help…"

"There you are, darlings!" Clara exclaimed from the doorway.

Arms outstretched, obviously more than tipsy, she staggered over to encircle them both with a single bear hug.

When she was finished, she stepped back. "Oh, my, Rosie, your man's even more of a looker than I remembered." She turned to Eddie and batted her eyes. "Seriously, you should become an actor."

He snorted.

"It's worth a try, anyway." She turned to Rosie. "Get ready for the girls to go gaga over him, honey." When she giggled, it sounded like a bell tinkling.

Rosie could feel a slight chill creep over her.

Oblivious, Clara took Rosie's hand. "Come, come, get yourselves drinks and meet my friends."

No sooner were they immersed in the throng, Eddie got nabbed by several stunning flappers with "Orchid Bob" hairdos, ruby red lips, and shifts that were almost transparent. Led off by Clara, Rosie looked back to see Eddie surrounded by a harem, his hands shielding himself from their pets and strokes, his face taking on a how-do-I-get-out-of-this look.

"Rosie, you ain't gonna get the hoity-toity crowd here today. Just us real folks," Clara said, cupping her cherubic mouth with both hands to magnify her words. On either side of them streamed an endless supply of people entering the house.

Hope we aren't squeezed to death.

"Well, well, well," a male voice sounded behind her. Turning around she saw the cameraman, Pete Roberts, his face puffy, his brow dotted with beads of sweat.

"Where's Eddie?" he yelled. His lips locked into a sneer.

She looked around. "I don't know. He seems to have disappeared."

"His loss, my gain," he said.

"What? I couldn't hear what you said."

He leaned in close, put his arm around her waist, and breathed into her ear. "I'm glad I got you alone," he said.

That time she heard him clear as a bell. Instinctively, she stepped back as Clara laughed.

"Honey, I don't know what he said to you, but just soak up the male attention," the actress said. Then she looked at Rosie's flushed cheeks and nervous eyes. "Hey, I'm sorry, kid. Come with me. Let's grab us a little quiet."

Armed with a new bottle of gin, the star steered them into one of the many bathrooms. Inside, she quickly locked the door.

"Drink up, sweetie," Clara directed.

She did, and when the gin flowed down her gullet, she coughed at the burn. She stared at the star, taking in that amazingly expressive face. Large eyes enhanced by pencil thin eyebrows, sienna eye shadow, and ruby painted lips met her gaze.

"I don't know why, but I feel comfortable with you, Rosie. More than most people. There are a lot of snakes around here in Hollywood; they just don't understand me." She took several swigs from the bottle and handed it over to her guest. "Tell me about yourself. What was your childhood like?"

"Nothing much to tell. I'm from Omaha, and according to my mother, my father, after fooling around with many different women, left us when I was young. Basically, she never got over that. Boring story, I'm sure."

Clara shook her head vigorously. "Not at all. There are things about my childhood that'd put even more curls on your head." She took a huge swig, and looked at Rosie with a sudden frown. "My mother was plumb crazy. We lived in the worst part of Brooklyn you could imagine, in a tenement with no hot water and no toilet, where people dropped their drawers and went whenever and wherever they felt like. Needless to say, the daily stench was not to be believed."

She placed her delicate hand on top of Rosie's arm. "See, kid? You can come from dirt and still make it big." She searched Rosie's face. "If you want to, that is."

"Making it in showbiz is Mama's dream, not mine." Rosie took a hefty nip of gin and wiped her mouth with the back of her hand. "After Papa left, the only thing that seemed to cheer Mama up was the movies. She just adored them and dragged me with her to so many of them. Basically, I grew up on Max Sennett, Charlie Chaplin, Harold Lloyd, Fatty Arbuckle, Gloria Swanson, you name it."

Clara nodded. "Me, too. Those flicks saved my life, I can tell you that. Several times a week, there I was, taking in those stars, staring at the screen and thinking that someday this was gonna be me."

"Not me. All I really ever loved were animals. You probably should've had my mama instead of yours. You'd have made her so happy by now."

In spite of their joint chuckle, Rosie sensed a definite sadness behind Clara's gaiety.

"So, what's with your guy, Rosie? Is he the one?" Clara downed more gin.

Did Rosie hear envy in her voice? If so, why in the world would someone like Clara envy anyone, much less a struggling actress? "He's a good guy, but…"

"No buts, Rosie. I ain't no 'Dumb Dora,' and you shouldn't be, neither. Grab on to any happiness you can. You don't want to wake up someday and regret things you could've had, but didn't out of fear. That's my motto, anyway." She blinked back tears.

Both a pounding on the door and a "Hey! Open up, I gotta go!" broke the mood.

"Well, enough reminiscing. Let's get outta here," the star said, her lights-camera-action face back full force.

As she went for the doorknob, she suddenly grabbed Rosie's arm. "Promise me you'll listen to your heart, Rosie. It'll tell you what to do."

It was Rosie's turn to have moist eyes. "But what if my heart's too confused right now?"

Clara shrugged. "Truth is, we're all a little lost. I figure my challenge in life was making it big. I guess listening to your heart will be yours," she said and unlocked the door.

As soon as the two women parted ways, Rosie began a search for Eddie. The noise level in each room made her head feel as if it were stuffed with cotton, and now, crushed against all of humanity once again, she had trouble concentrating. Tipsy, she tried to edge her way through each room, bit-by-bit, feeling like someone lost at sea, fighting oncoming waves. When a man grabbed her arm and swung her around, she almost fainted.

It was Pete Roberts again, still staggering, now almost purple-faced. This time he was holding a wad of cash. "See this, Rosie?" he asked, fumes of whiskey from his breath blasting toward her face. "This is from a bet I had with some of the fellers. And I won." His grin reminded her of the Cheshire cat in *Alice in Wonderland.*

She wanted to shove him off, but his grip was too strong. "What bet?" she sneered, bending back as far away from him as she could.

"I bet the guys that the newest shooter was the same man who killed Harris. Your Eddie!"

"What?" she half screamed. "What are you talking about?"

He beamed, obviously thrilled at her reaction. "He was missing right when it happened on the set, wasn't he? He had trouble with the producer, didn't he?" He leaned in close. "Where was he last night when another shooting happened, huh? With you? If he wasn't, then it's anyone's guess where he was."

She had trouble breathing. No, it couldn't be Eddie. He was with Lon. Or was he? He had seemed so evasive in the car when she talked to him. And why hadn't he called? Why—

"Cat got your tongue, Rosie?"

She drew herself up. "Yes, Pete, he was with me. Let go of my arm and go away. You're disgusting!"

His eyes registered hurt, still, he loosened his grip. But when he saw her looking over at Eddie in a nearby corner, he got upset. Spitting out a harsh "Dammit!" he staggered off.

"Rosie!" Eddie yelled through the din. He had his sweater and tie off by this time and seemed upset, even though he was surrounded by a bevy of at least five girls, rubbing his arms and chest in the most indecent way. Clinging to him, they were like monkeys on a tree. As Rosie watched him trying to extricate himself from their collective grip, it was obvious all his earlier politeness had gone out the window. He wrenched himself free of their hold and almost knocked one of them down. Then, using shoulder block after shoulder block, he made his way over to her to draw her into his arms.

"Thank God, I saw you," he called into her ear. "Where have you been? I've been looking for you everywhere! You left me with all these insane girls! Let's go home. I've had enough."

In spite of her general fear of losing him, in spite of Beatrice's warnings inside her head, she let the gin take over and allowed herself to just feel. How grand it was to be crunched up against his taut, strapping body, to know she was the special prize he chose over all those girls she had seen gravitating to him like hummingbirds to nectar. Never had she felt so attracted to him than at that moment. Forgotten were Pete Roberts' accusations, gone all her usual insecurities. There was only an overwhelming urge to go somewhere private together.

The night was coming on strong as they started off. Darkness blended with a full, gauzy moon, creating an eerie, yet beautiful glow. Like the murkiness of a night film shoot set near a lagoon, she told him. When he nodded thoughtfully, she took it further. She suggested that since it was still somewhat early and a lovely night, why didn't they drive up into the Hollywood hills via Mulholland Drive?

Slowly, they wound their way along the untraveled road, higher and higher. Up ahead they saw a large medieval-esque house, sparse in both ground foliage and houses nearby.

"That's Harry Houdini's home," Eddie said as they climbed still higher toward the Hollywoodland sign.

With no street lamps present, Eddie's yellow headlights were the only things visible besides the stars, until they saw something beyond the horizon. Two bright beams of white were crisscrossed up into the sky.

"There must be a new movie opening at the Egyptian Theater," he said, staring at the beams shifting. "Ah, the wonders of Hollywood." She didn't answer and after a couple more minutes of a dim road he asked, "Where do you want to go?"

She edged closer to him on the seat. "Somewhere magical, where we can put down a blanket and overlook the world."

He chuckled. "I know just the spot," he said and drove on. Soon, they reached a summit where the road could only go down toward the farms and orange groves of San Fernando Valley on the other side. "Good enough for you? See? With all the lights down below in Hollywood and the stars above, we can pretend we're halfway to Heaven."

Still somewhat wobbly, she got out and approached the ridge. Like a shot, he bolted out of the car and over to her, placing his arm around her shoulder in a protective hold. Below them Hollywood looked like a blanket of flickering jewels, blinking softly.

"Looks like the tinsel my parents used to put on our Christmas tree," he said gently. "Glad you suggested this. I've been meaning to talk to you anyway."

"Can we sit and watch for a while?" Rosie asked, ignoring his last sentence.

"Sure, I'll get a blanket. Stay there and don't go any closer to the edge."

She giggled.

"I *mean* it, Rosie," he added.

She stood stock still, her arms plastered to her side in a comedic come-to-attention army stance.

When he returned, he carefully tested for a soft spot with one toe of his boot then lowered the blanket onto the grass. Immediately she plopped down on it and steadied herself, *Hold me,* the only thing on her mind.

"Kiss me, Eddie," she said, her voice sounding like velvet.

His gasp came out like a deep groan. He was on the blanket in an instant, pulling her close.

After months of enjoying their secret sessions, and now, fueled by gin and Clara's last words to her, new sensations cropped up in her body. She craved much more than just being held. His kisses on her neck were sparking tingle after tingle up and down her arms. As his hands roamed down her back and waist, her arms wrapped around him so fast, so instinctively, she gasped. His kiss on her lips, always sensuous before, now felt much deeper, more probing. And she loved it. No thoughts of other girls or whether or not he was there for her. He was simply there, making her ache for him to touch her most private parts—parts she had protected well, until now.

"Rosie, Rosie," he murmured in between kisses, "you're so beautiful."

"Eddie, take me now. Forget about candles and a real bed. I want you."

He sat up with a grunt. "You sure? I don't want to do anything…"

"I need it now," she moaned and pulled him back down onto her.

Beatrice had never explained the facts of life to her, but she had heard enough from the other girls to know it was going to hurt the first time. Still, she was willing to take a chance. It was Eddie, not some fumbling stranger. No doubt he would know what to do.

And he did. He skillfully pulled her dress down off her shoulders, and as soon as his hand cupped first one breast, then the other, she arched her torso upward so she could melt into him, as if they were one. Pulling up her skirt, he started fingering her, and instantly, she forgot everything else. Her soft moans of pleasure seemed to come from someone else. Certainly, not from the defensive girl who would never let any man harm her.

"Oh, Rosie," he hissed and continued to touch her, until she exploded into wave after wave of pleasure.

When she finished, she noticed he paused, as if he was waiting for her to recover.

Her heart still pounding, her breaths jerky and uneven, she managed an "Oh, my."

His sigh sounded shaky as well. "Yeah," he said simply.

Through her haze, she placed her hand on his chest. "Don't you want to make love to me?"

"Of course," he growled. Yet his eyes hinted at something else. Protectiveness? Locked in a glow of satiation, she couldn't quite tell. "I just don't want to hurt you," he added.

"Do, it, oh, please do it!" she moaned, the sudden urge for more release washing over her.

He pulled away to sit up. No longer draped on top of her, she felt chilled, almost bereaved. But the sound of his belt unbuckling came next, and then he was on top of her, whispering, "I'll be gentle, Rosie, I promise."

Later, they stayed curled up together on the blanket, listening to all the night sounds—an owl who-whoing, crickets sawing, and a lone coyote off in the distance, baying its plaintive song at the moon.

"You know, being an actress wasn't ever my dream," she said. "The truth is, I don't think I'm even good at it."

He chuckled. "Well, I know one thing you're good at." He nibbled on her ear. "You're a natural at this, Rosie."

She could feel her cheeks warming in embarrassment. "Oh, Eddie, please, I'm a good girl. I don't know what came over me."

"It's called love-making—the way it's supposed to be." He continued his soft caresses on her neck.

She could feel her chest tightening. "Let's not talk about it anymore."

It was as if he didn't hear her. "Just think, we could do this all the time if we were married. That's what I wanted to talk to you about. Let me take you away from all this…this Glamour Town."

A swirl of thoughts suddenly erupted in her. Relief that he truly wanted her wrestled with Beatrice's hostility toward him and her father's total disloyalty, once married.

She pushed away from him and sat up. "We should probably get home. Mama's gonna have a kitten if we don't."

From below her she heard him give a deep sigh. "Oh, Rosie," he murmured, but she didn't care.

They adjusted their clothes, picked up the blanket and drove off without a single word between them.

To Rosie, huddled against her car door, the trip back seemed to take forever. Or at least there was plenty of time for her mind to run its usual rapid pace. This time, the image of Pete Roberts and his wad of cash played a starring role, along with her mama's sour face whenever Eddie's name was mentioned. *Am I gonna have my dream tonight?* She began to bite her nails just before they pulled up to the Highland Courts.

There were Walt and Beatrice, both sitting outside on the stoop. Immediately, Beatrice stood up, crossed her arms and glowered, while Walt sneaked a swig from his flask. They both watched Rosie get out of the car after Eddie opened her door.

"Look, Rosie," he said softly, then hesitated. "I shouldn't have said anything. I know how scared you get, but please try and remember this one thing. Just 'cause your father took a powder, that's doesn't mean I'm going to. Why, I—"

She put a finger on his lips, her tears already in place. "Don't. I just can't talk right now. I don't know why, but I can't. Please, can't we just leave it at that?"

CHAPTER ELEVEN

*"If at first you don't succeed, try, try again. Then quit.
There's no point in being a damn fool about it."*
— W. C. Fields, actor

January 23, 1926
Nineteen Days AFTER the Harris Murder

FRANK STARED DOWN at the three different morning newspapers fanned out across his desk.

"STILL NO ARRESTS"
"ANOTHER HOLLYWOOD KILLING?"
"WHERE ARE THE POLICE?"

Each giant headline before him hammered home a single fact, one that kept him up late and helped to set off his nightly inebriation. The Harris killer was still on the loose, and to top it off, this newest murder had created total havoc in the Hollywood police station. He kept thinking about a mob connection. At least with this latest one. And the other rifle killings? Maybe the mob as well. If so, which source could he use to find out more? Eyes shut now, locked in concentration, he suddenly thought of someone. *Bruno Ricci. Yeah, he might know something.*

"You look like hell," Shire had told him as soon as he came in.

Later, when Frank went to the bathroom and splashed some water onto his face, he glanced at his reflection in the mirror, and he had to agree. He looked like one of those lost souls at Sister Aimee McPherson's church, waiting in line to be fed.

It was the first time he could remember when his fellow cops were actually doing their jobs—walking their beats, knocking on doors, and comparing notes. Still, he had a sinking feeling in his gut. No matter what, someone would be arrested and charged, whether he'd done it or not. That was simply the *modus operandi* of the Los Angeles police force these days.

Of course, Billings demanded to see him. Lately, that seemed to have become a pattern Frank would love to break. *What is it this time?* Bitter thoughts crowded his mind as he entered the captain's office and took a seat.

"I'm gonna give it to you straight, Lozano," Billings began.

Lozano shifted uncomfortably in his chair. *Not a good sign.* "Oh?"

"Yeah, since you've indicated you aren't willing to go the extra mile here, I've got Detective Williams to do your job."

"And that would be—?" Frank said slowly, knowing full well what Williams probably had planted in Eddie's car.

"Don't be such a smart aleck," Billings grunted. "Williams is young and hungry for promotion." He peered over at Frank. "Something you've obviously left behind at the barstool." There was a pause. "Anyway, I sent him out to do what you should have done a while ago. You know, regarding our discussion about a certain suspect in the Harris case?" He gave a dismissive hand wave. "Just thought you should know. You can go now."

When Frank returned to his desk, Shire immediately asked, "What's up?"

Frank sank down in his chair, his shoulders hunched. "The wheels of justice turning, is all," he said grimly and reached into his jacket pocket to pull out his flask.

That same morning, on the other side of town, when Eddie again admitted to Mabel at breakfast about his confusion and frustration with Rosie, he failed to mention the flashbacks he had been experiencing recently. Several images of Maggie with a stunned look on her face after his careless treatment of her had popped up. After all these years, how could his guilt still affect him so much?

"I won't let Rosie down, I won't," he muttered, ignoring the breakfast of eggs, bacon, and toast set before him.

His landlady planted her palm firmly down on the table. "Eddie, there's no two ways about it. You're a honey lamb, and if Rosie can't see that, that's her misfortune. Maybe it's time to move on. After all, she—" Mabel never finished. He had already risen, and with a set jaw, left without a word.

Outside, as he went to his car, he noticed the warm sun had brought with it a pleasant breeze. He took a deep breath. *I shouldn't have been so curt with Mabel. Must apologize later.*

Just then, Mabel called out to him from the porch with a goodbye wave. "A fine Los Angeles day in the making. Have a great one, honey!"

He smiled back at her, waved, and started his car and headed toward Lon's. With his mentor's automobile in the shop, Eddie had been playing chauffeur service for several days now. Shoving all ruminations aside, he concentrated on his accelerator and started off.

He drove only fifteen yards.

Suddenly, an unmarked car careened sideways in front of him, blocking his path. Stunned, Eddie watched with alarm as two men dressed in cheap suits hopped out of the car. With their weapons drawn, they pointed their Colt Model M's at him.

"Eddie Willis, put your hands up and get out of the car. Now!" one of them bellowed.

Off in the distance, Eddie could hear Mabel hollering, "What's going on?"

His hands raised, he slowly got out of the car. But before he could finish saying, "What's this all about?" one of the men had him slammed up against the car hood, his face pressed so hard against the metal, he could feel his jaw click.

Next came the cold, tight clasp of swing handcuffs—first on his right wrist, then his left, with his shoulders being strained back far enough to bring on stabs of pain.

Mabel had reached them by that point. "What the hell is going on? Why in the world are you arresting this man?"

Meanwhile, the other police officer rummaged around in Eddie's car, obviously looking for something. *But what?* Eddie's heartbeats galloped.

"I don't understand. Are you arresting me?" he asked, his nostrils flared.

The cop searching in the car stepped out and held up a shell casing. "What is this, Willis, huh?"

Eddie stared in disbelief. "Hey, that's not mine." He paused, his mind whirling. "Someone's planted that in my car," he insisted. Detective Lozano's face popped into his mind. "And I know who did it!"

"Oh, you do, do you? Too bad, Willis. You're coming down with us to headquarters for a little chat."

Both men jerked him toward the police car as Mabel ran up to them.

"Stay back, Mabel!" Eddie cried. "I don't want you to get hurt. Just call Lon and tell him, all right?"

Mabel looked as though she was about to land a punch on the closest cop's jaw.

"Mabel! You hear me? Just get Lon," Eddie repeated, before he was roughly shoved down into the police car.

Frank noticed Eddie had a black eye as soon as they brought him in. A real ringer by the looks of it. Either he fought back, or the police got tough just for the heck of it. When Eddie was unceremoniously thrown into the station's cell, and Frank saw Williams across the room, pantomiming a strong jab to several other detectives, he knew the answer. *Definitely a gift from the Los Angeles police department.*

Frank knew enough to stay away from the prisoner. The one time he did look back at the cell, Eddie was eyeballing him with such ferocity he automatically turned back to his desk to do paperwork.

The room was buzzing with noise—typewriters clacking, the secretaries talking to the different men on the floor, and Billings, who, with a grin the size of Kansas, loudly called Williams into his office.

I'm through here. Instantly, Frank's familiar cravings cropped up, superseding everything else. He was about to stand up and tell Shire he had had it and was going out for a drink, when he saw a small entourage of four men march into the station, demanding to speak to the "person in charge."

Three of the men were dressed in expensive suits. One man, with a vaguely familiar face, was in a plain jacket. Frank stood and watched, waffling between getting something numbing down his gullet and waiting to see who that person was. Then it dawned on him. It was Lon Chaney, actor and makeup artist extraordinaire. Right here in person!

There was no way on earth he was going to miss this, so instead of leaving, he casually got up and sauntered over to the tiny coffee room next to the sergeant's office. Positioned just on the other side of Billing's wall, over time Frank had realized it held a treasure. A small vent down near the floorboards between the two rooms helped him be privy to a whole host of secrets emanating from the captain's private office. Secrets that had served him well in the past, and might now once again.

Sticking his head out into the main room to make sure no one was watching him, he pulled back and knelt down in front of the vent. With one ear up near the grill, he listened.

The lawyers were obviously doing their job. "This is absurd, Captain Billings. My client claims that shell casing did not belong to him," one man said, his voice crisp, cold, efficient.

"That's what he would say, isn't it?" came Billings' smug-sounding reply. Frank could just picture the smirk on his boss's lips.

Several huffs and grunts followed. Then, "I'm Mr. Willis' employer, and I'm here not only to attest to his whereabouts, I can also vouch for his character. It is impeccable."

Billings made a quick comment. "So, you're saying, then, Mr. Chaney, that you knew every second where he was on the day that Chester Harris was shot and killed?"

"Well, no. I was not on the set at the time," the celebrity said slowly.

"Apparently, numerous people claim Mr. Willis was not actually there when the bullet hit the deceased. Mr. Willis himself even admitted he wasn't there, saying he had run an errand for the victim. He also owns a similar rifle as the shooter."

There was a prolonged pause. Then came another remark from Billings. "What do you have to say about that, Mr. Chaney, hmm?"

Chaney's tone sounded clipped. "I know Mr. Willis well, and I believe whatever he has to say."

"You do, do you?" Billings was in high gear and obviously enjoying himself. Frank had seen him in action before. "How about the other night with another murder by a sniper? Mr. Willis claims he was with you. Is that true?"

"Yes, he sure was. He was helping me take my wife to the hospital, since my car had broken down the day before. You can check with the doctor who treated her, if you don't believe me."

"Oh, I shall, Mr. Chaney, I shall. Perhaps you would also care to elaborate about the rifle that Mr. Willis keeps in his room. The same kind of rifle that was used on Mr. Harris."

Another voice popped up, tinged with anger. "Captain. I don't think you realize who my client, Mr. Chaney, is. He's a person who is quite powerful in Hollywood. I don't think you want to mess with the consequences of getting into an entanglement with the studios, now, do you? Release Mr. Willis now."

Lots of chairs scraping against wood came next. Frank stood up, but when he heard Billings clear his throat, he leaned down again and cocked his ear to the vent, to hear what else his boss had to add.

"All right, you've won this round, but it is within my rights to question Mr. Willis one more time before he goes. You can remain here, but more questions will be asked. And by the way, I've been in touch with Medford. They just want this whole thing cleared up. Williams, bring in the prisoner. Now."

Soon, there were more shuffling noises, as if more people had entered the room.

"Eddie, the captain here wants to ask you more questions," someone said. Frank assumed it was a lawyer who hadn't spoken before.

"Like what?" It was clearly Eddie's voice now, deep and sounding fully incensed.

"Like I want to hear again why you weren't present on the Harris set at the time of the shooting."

"Captain Billings, my client has already told you and your people about that. This is absurd, and frankly, a waste of our time. We're done here."

The slow scraping of chairs could be heard again, giving Frank time to get out of the coffee room and head back to his desk.

Turning to watch them all leave, Frank was surprised to see Eddie stop and say something to Lon Chaney, then make a visual sweep of the squad room. As soon as he spotted Frank, despite one of his lawyers' attempt to pull him back, he came charging over to the detective.

Eyes flashing, hands fisted, Eddie stepped in close. "I know why you're really after me."

"Oh yeah? Why, wise guy?"

His entourage appeared, and Lon put an arm on his shoulder. "Let's go, Eddie. They have nothing on you, you hear me? Nothing."

Shifting forward, Eddie started to go off with his group, but at the last minute, he swung back to Frank. He got in the detective's face. "Rosie," he hissed. Then he turned and left with the others.

Frank sat down at his desk. *Damn. Willis is smarter than I thought. Yeah, exactly. With him out of the way...*

He could feel Shire studying him, knew he was bound to get an acerbic comment later from his partner. But for now, he lit up a cigarette and watched Eddie leave. As a large cloud of smoke swirled up and around him, he sat still, deep in thought. *Yeah, Rosie...*

"Well?" Shire asked.

"Well, I'm off," Frank said simply and stood up.

"Where to?"

"Something I gotta take care of," he said. "Two things, actually."

Frank knew exactly where his source, Bruno Ricci, would be—a dumpy speakeasy called House of Sin. To add insult to injury, it was located in the basement of a local church. It was anyone's guess what possessed the pastor to allow that, but to Frank, it was obvious. Money. Moulah. Cash. Whatever you wanted to call it.

The detective wasn't a religious man, yet it did feel somewhat sacrilegious to lightly tread through the peaceful church, passing a few prayerful worshipers on his way to a side door up near the front. Once opened, Frank proceeded down two flights, like going to the bowels of the earth. Dank, musky, the walls reeked from decades of mold. Finally, he came face-to-face with a heavy iron door. *Looks like the gate to a medieval torture chamber.*

Ramming the heavy iron knocker twice, it was opened by a hunched over, decrepit old man, as plumes of cigarette smoke instantly bombarded them both. Inside, unlike his beloved Shifty's, this place had with it an eerie silence that was louder than any of the fast jive rhythms he was used to. Here, the customers quietly imbibed in their drinks slowly, steadily, as if to thoroughly drown out their sorrows, or at the very least, wash away the world.

Sure enough, Bruno was there, sitting on a barstool, coveting a cluster of empty shot glasses lined up in front of him. When Frank swung one leg after another over the stool next to the Italian snitch, he immediately slapped the man on the back.

"How's things, Bruno?" he asked.

Bruno looked up and over at him, his eyes glazed. He tried to make a finger salute, but his finger missed its mark and almost poked his eye.

Frank shook his head. *Oh, boy, he's not gonna be any good to me.*

"What brings you here?" Ricci asked, his slurred words sounding more like Italian than English.

Here goes. "I wonder if you know anything about the Harris murder?"

Ricci nodded. "Sure."

Frank leaned in inches from the man's bloated face. "And?"

"I heard Ardizzone hired a hit man."

"Yeah? Who?"

"And talk is Harris' aide, what's his name, that pipsqueak also made some kinda payoff."

"Henry Blake?" *I knew that jerk had guilty written all over him.* "Well, which one did it?"

The canary shrugged. "Who knows?"

Damn. Frank sighed, patted the man's back again, and took off to his second destination. *I swear, I'm gonna follow that Blake guy, anyway. I smell a big rat.*

So far, Rosie had had a bad day. Although she was given a bigger part than usual on the set of *The American Venus*—she even got to be up front in one of the scenes—her mind and heart just weren't into it.

Eddie's and her lovemaking had released so much passion in her, she was left stunned. Who knew sex could be so grand? Whenever Rosie thought of her parents together, they never touched each other or appeared to be close. Being young when her father had left, she never questioned any of that. It wasn't until she was much older that she heard Beatrice say over sudsy dishwater one night, when she thought she was alone, "Don't know what's so great about sex, anyway."

On the set now, she had mixed feelings about seeing Eddie. She knew he was slated to be present that day, but again, she felt confused. Ashamed of her cold reaction to him at the end of the night conflicted with a need to see him again, to possibly touch him, if only in passing.

But he wasn't there, and as the day progressed, she grew worried. Was he avoiding her? Had he finally had enough and decided not to continue their relationship? She could feel herself drifting toward the same anxiety she had experienced as a child each time her father would leave for a day or so, without a word.

The director's last, "Cut! That's it for the day, everyone," startled her out of her thoughts. As they all filed out onto the street, she prayed she might at least see Eddie's car. But it wasn't there. Instead, she noticed Detective Lozano leaning against his car, watching her like a hawk coveting its prey. She could sense her pulse rising. *Why won't that man leave us alone?*

He came over and stood in front of her, a foot and a half away. "Hello, Miss Paige. Got a minute?"

She nodded. "What's this about, detective?"

"Eddie Willis."

Her pupils grew large. "What about him?"

"We need to talk. Can we go somewhere private?"

"Like where? Is Eddie all right?"

Ignoring her question, he asked. "How 'bout the Shadow Café, around the corner? I can't do it now, but tonight at seven?"

She stiffened. "You mean like a date?"

"No, no, of course not," he said quickly. "It's just business."

"All right, then. Seven. But tell me about Eddie. Where is he?"

"I'm not at liberty to—" He saw her put her hand to her throat. "Well, all right. He was questioned today at headquarters."

"Why? Why?" She felt a rising panic.

He stepped even closer. "I can tell you only one thing. Maybe the rest later."

"What one thing?"

"Eddie didn't have an alibi for this past Sunday night. Were you with him?"

"No. He said he was with Lon. He…" she trailed off.

Frank's eyes narrowed. "All right then. See you tonight at seven." He tapped his finger to his brim in a goodbye gesture then walked off.

The Shadow Café had seen better days. The original light tan sawdust sprinkled across its wooden floor now had a darkish hue to it. According to Frank, one could almost say the same for the food served there. Home to cheerful crowds a mere two years ago, its patrons had recently become far and few in-between. Still, there was a reason Frank stayed loyal to the place. The owner, Gus, an old friend, was perfectly willing to look the other way when the detective sat in his favorite booth in the murkiest corner of the restaurant. It was there, under cover of darkness, that he could take out his flask and pour gin into his glass, and no one would be the wiser.

Knowing he was going to meet up with Rosie that night, he'd made sure to arm himself with two flasks of gin, instead of his usual single vessel. One in each pocket. It wouldn't hurt to get her a little pickled. *Damn.* He found himself getting more excited than he had in months.

At seven-ten she was still a no-show. Same thing at seven-twenty. Frank took several fast swigs. *Where the hell is she?*

When she finally appeared at seven-thirty, his pulse double-timed. Her day costume ditched, she was wearing a floral V-neck dress in true flapper fashion. He stood up and strode over to her.

"Didn't think you were gonna come."

"Sorry, detective, I had trouble getting away. Finally, I just told my mother I was meeting a friend."

Frank nodded. "I see."

"So, what about Eddie?" she asked.

"Please, come with me." He gently yet firmly cupped her elbow and led her back to his table. He noticed when she walked he could hear the swish of her dress brush against her stockings and against her waist and breasts. *Wow.*

As soon as they sat down, she laid her arms on the table with her fingers intertwined. "So, tell me what's going on about Eddie. He wasn't home earlier when I tried to call him."

"Please, you seem agitated. Why don't you have something to drink before we get into it?"

She looked around. "Here? At a restaurant, not a speakeasy? How's that possible?"

Grinning, he took out one of his flasks and poured some gin in each of the glasses Gus had provided for them. "The owner and I go way back. Don't worry. No one will notice us. I guarantee it."

Again, she looked around. "Of course, they won't. There's nobody here but us."

Ah, there's that quick wit again. He noted her cupid-shaped mouth.

"Please tell me about Eddie."

"Drink up first."

When she raised her glass, he contemplated her neck. *So kissable.* He swilled his drink down.

After she daintily swallowed, she stroked her throat, as if to ease the burn from the alcohol. He quickly poured more into her emptied glass.

"Maybe you should set your goals higher. None of that low-level stuff." he said.

"What do you mean?"

"I'm talking about Eddie," he said. "As I told you before, he is now a prime suspect."

"I just can't believe it, I can't. I *know* him. He wouldn't do something like that."

"Miss Paige—Rosie—in the end, do we really know people?" he asked cynically.

She guzzled her next drink down so fast, he could see her head begin to sway. *Uh-oh. Maybe getting her half-seas-over drunk wasn't such a good idea.*

"If Eddie says he was with Lon on Sunday, he was. I'm sure of it," she said, her voice a mix of nervousness and defiance. She pushed her glass toward him. "More, please."

Hesitating, he sighed.

"More," she repeated, her eyes already glassy.

He took out his spare flask and poured a little in her glass.

"Fill it up, please." No doubt about it. She was already hammered.

He complied. *Oh, boy.* She was obviously reeling.

"What else do you have for me, detective…detective…"

She can't even remember my name. "Frank. Listen, Rosie, it's not important. I shouldn't have—"

"No-no-no! You started this. Tell me what else you got."

His sigh seemed to last forever. "Well, when I visited him, he had a rifle."

"And?" She pushed her glass out toward him again.

He shook his head. "You've had enough. This rifle, it was the same make as the one used to kill Harris."

He waited for that to sink in, expecting more indignation toward him. But there wasn't any. Instead, her eyes filled with tears, and she cupped one hand over her mouth.

"Oh my God," she whispered, as tears slid down her cheeks. "I can't believe it. Eddie's always been so kind, so patient, so gentle."

He said nothing.

"I come from a broken home, you know, with lots of disappointments. But Eddie didn't care. He was always there for me. He…" Choking sobs took over.

Frank put out his hand. She grabbed it and gazing into his eyes, said the worst possible thing for him to hear. "What would I do without him?" she moaned.

Shame washed over him. "Rosie…"

"What?" she asked, so far gone, she seemed to be looking past him.

"Time to get you home. Don't worry about anything. Just get some sleep."

As soon as Beatrice saw them at the curb, she burst out of the apartment complex and marched over to Frank's car. Walt had come out as well, but stayed fixed under the court's archway, arms folded, frowning.

"Where have you been, young lady?" Beatrice demanded. "I thought you were with a friend. What's going on?" She turned to Frank. "Detective Lozano, right?"

"Yes, that's right, Mrs. Paige. Look, it's my fault. I needed to talk to her about the Harris case."

"I can smell gin a mile away. Is that how you question people these days, detective?"

He shook his head. "No, of course not. My apologies."

"Rosie, get inside right now." She turned and stalked back toward the complex.

Left alone with the actress, Frank said. "Rosie, sorry. Like I said, just get some sleep." He watched Walt walk away. "By the way, who is that man?"

She looked over at the retreating figure, and lurched toward Frank. He caught her and held her upright.

"That's Walt, our super," she managed. "He's like family. He's great. He—I don't feel so well." She suddenly leaned over and vomited all over the grass and his shoes.

"That's it." He scooped her up and carried her toward the Paige apartment.

An irate Beatrice was firmly planted at their front door. "Put her down, detective. You've done quite enough tonight. I'll take it from here."

"Again, I'm sorry, Mrs. Paige."

She nodded curtly as he tipped his hat goodnight. After an awkward silence, he turned to leave. *I guess there's nothing more to say.*

But he was wrong. When he turned to go, he swore he heard Beatrice mutter, "Men. Damn them all to hell."

CHAPTER TWELVE

*"I felt like they only cared about what I could do
for them, not what they could do for me."*
— Norma Talmadge, actress

**January 24, 1926
Twenty Days AFTER the Harris Shooting
The Morning after Frank's Meeting with Rosie**

IN 1919, WHEN majestic battleships needed a good home before heading over to Europe and the Great War, San Diego Bay was deemed too shallow. San Pedro, however, was not, and before long, ships and other small crafts were docked there in what was fast becoming a thriving seaport, with several warehouses and a few fisheries. A mere twenty-one miles away from downtown Los Angeles, word soon circulated about secret underground tunnels, perfect for the City Hall Gang's bootlegging organizations, and Tony Cornero's rum-running business.

Frank was no fool. Bruno Ricci and others had told him over the years about the secret underground thoroughfares and how these above ground warehouses were a gold mine of well-stocked liquor boxes, ready for transportation orders from the likes of Charles H. Crawford and his chum, Kent Kane Parrot, the co-founders of City Hall Gang.

Today, that was the least of Frank's concerns. He simply wanted to be up close and personal—and if necessary, threaten—a couple of Crawford's "soldiers" to find out anything new and real about the Harris killing.

The weather was spectacular, and if he hadn't had such a determined mindset, he might have enjoyed just sitting on the dock, watching the various boats float in, as he inhaled the sea air.

Parked near a warehouse he knew to be secretly owned by the Ardizzone gang, he suddenly recognized a couple of men he had encountered during his early police days, before the police department had been retained by the mob and the crooked Crawford-Parrot politicos.

Hello, here they come. Two toughies, wearing newsboy hats and dressed in dusty pants, vests, collarless shirts with rolled up sleeves ambled by his car. He got out and casually followed them around the corner. When one of them stopped to light up his cig, Frank took over.

"Hey, you work for the Iron Man, right?"

They both exchanged looks.

"Don't know who you're talking about," the heavier of the two said.

Frank smiled. "Joseph Iron Man Ardizzone, and I think you know that."

The other man, on-the-thin-side, gulped. "What's it to you? What are you, a cop?"

Frank produced his badge.

"Hell," the fat one muttered.

"Yeah, you better tell me something about the Chester Harris murder or hell will come down on you."

"I don't know anything about—"

In a flash, Frank shoved the slender man against an iron fence and wrapped his hand around the guy's throat. "Cough up something or else," he snarled.

"Leave him alone!" the heavy one shouted. "He don't know nothing. But I do."

Relaxing his hold, Frank turned. "Well?" he asked.

"It's true. I heard there was a contract out on Harris. Some young nobody was to do it, too." The chunky man handed his friend his dirty handkerchief.

"A name. Give me a name," Frank ordered.

"Honest to God, I wish I knew. But I'll tell you something else, but you didn't hear it from me."

Frank scratched his head. "Yeah, what?"

"I heard that Harris' boyfriend was also out to get him. Paid off someone for it, too."

"Again, names."

"Hey, detective, I'm just giving you hearsay. I ain't got no details. Leave us alone, will ya?"

Watching them both run off, Frank got back into his car, took several gulps out of his flask, and sat thinking. *Damn. Back to square one—two main suspects. And Eddie? Oh, boy, that's a tough one.*

When the little girl pushes against the gray door, to her surprise, it swings open easily and so completely, it strikes the wall behind it with a thump. The girl laughs with delight. Pleased with her sudden power, she embarks on her familiar journey—to see what's inside the house. This time there are no noises behind her. No sirens blaring, no man claiming he'll help her. Only an eerie silence.

She steps forward, cautious, yet energized. Unlike the semi-lit room where she had faced a monster, here, there is a male figure in front of a blazing fire, with his back to her.

"Can you help me?" she asks, not feeling quite as empowered as she did before.

The man slowly rotates around. Dark-haired, he is without features—no eyes, nose, or lips. Startled, she falls backward, but he is quick on his feet. He rushes over to catch her. Then slowly, gently, he places her down on the room's sofa.

When he begins to leave, she calls out, "Who are you?" But he doesn't answer; he just exits without a word.

This time when Rosie woke up, it wasn't with a jolt. She felt no heart-pounding, no heavy sweats. Just a ferocious headache and hangover, as she woozily looked around her room with half-closed lids. Nestled around her neck lay Ginger, purring so loudly, it was as if a car motor was vibrating up into her head. Draped over her legs, Patches gave a long stretch then yawned with a tiny yip. She could hear Beatrice in the kitchen, spouting loudly about something.

Uh-oh. Mama's obviously furious—is it at me? Through a fog, she wracked her brain, trying to remember details about the night before, but she couldn't do it. She did remember she was with Detective Lozano at a restaurant. There was also a lot of gin, and a discussion about—

Eddie! It came back to her in a flash. According to Lozano, he was the prime suspect in the Harris case and now the Sunday shooting. No, it couldn't be.

Suddenly, nausea overcame her full force. As she staggered out to the bathroom, she could hear Beatrice's "Is that you, Rosie?" behind her.

Who else would it be? She sank down onto her knees, cradled the toilet bowl and heaved up everything from the night before.

Ten minutes later, cleaned up and somewhat refreshed, she shuffled into the kitchen, where a newspaper-absorbed Walt casually looked up and smiled. Beatrice was pouring coffee and made no move to acknowledge her.

Here we go.

"Rosie, here's some coffee," Beatrice finally said and handed her daughter the largest mug they owned, filled to the brim. "I'm sure you could use this."

That would definitely help.

"So. What do you have to say for yourself, young lady? Visiting a friend, indeed. Coming in drunk and with that man, that detective. As far as I'm concerned, he's no gentleman, even if he says he was interrogating you."

"Yeah, that doesn't hold water," Walt said, his brow furrowed. "As cops go, that's going over the edge."

"I agree," Beatrice said. "Do I have to set tighter reins on you, Rosie? I will, you know." She pointed to the *Los Angeles Herald's* front page. "I don't want you ending up like Clara Bow. Show her, Walt."

Walt held up the newspaper for her to see the headline: "Clara Bow Sure Enjoys Her Football Fellas!"

Rosie leaned in for a closer look. "What the—"

She saw how the Hearst paper had had a field day with the celebrity. According to the article, at her recent party, Clara had performed debasing sexual acts with each of the football players, one after another.

"Walt, why do you always have to load our kitchen table with all these newspapers?" Rosie asked, her voice sharp.

"Look, Rosie-Posey, I just wanted to—"

Beatrice butted in. "Leave Walt alone!"

Rosie shook her head. "Why in the world would they write that about her?"

"You're telling us it wasn't true?" Beatrice's voice dripped with disdain.

"Mama, of course not!"

"Well," Beatrice continued, "how do you know? Maybe while you and that Eddie were off doing things, she was having the time of her life. Multiple times, I might add."

Caught off guard, Rosie thought of Mulholland Drive at night and blushed.

Her mother's "warning finger" wagged. "Ah-hah! You were up to something no good. I knew I couldn't trust that too-handsome-for-his-own-good Eddie!"

When the phone rang, Beatrice got up to answer it. With Detective Lozano's warnings still ringing in her ears, her mother's nonstop disapproval embedded in her brain, Rosie reacted.

"If it's Eddie, please say I'm not here," she said.

Her mother paused. "Really?"

The phone rang several more times, then stopped. When it rang again, this time, Beatrice picked up the receiver and listened. Then, with the most triumphant look on her face, she said, "She's not here, Eddie. Please don't call again."

Sitting down again at the table, Beatrice's eyes were all lit up. "What's going on, Rosie, hmm? Finally got sick of him?"

"I don't want to discuss it."

Beatrice leaned forward. "I think—"

"Stop it! You don't always like to discuss things, Mama, and you know what? Right now, I don't want to, either. Please just leave me alone."

"I will say one thing, though," Beatrice said, "at least when you go to Gloria Swanson's party this weekend with Mr. Berns, I won't have to worry about you."

There he is, making another drop. With his car lights off, motor still purring, Frank watched Henry Blake meet up with someone outside of Fiorello's, a small Italian restaurant close to Medford Studios. Pete Roberts, the cameraman, was right. Whoever this man was, he didn't look like a mobster. A well-tailored jacket, trousers, vest, and bowtie all suggested something else. But what, exactly?

After Henry handed a thick, letter envelope over to the man, he got back into his car and took off. Meanwhile, Mr. Bowtie stayed put for several seconds. Then he shoved the wadded envelope deep into his pants' pocket and climbed into another car. Once his starter essentials were pushed and cranked, he quickly drove away.

Nice ride. A Chrysler 1924 Model B-70. More than curious now, Frank waited until the man's spiffy automobile was halfway down the block before the detective turned his lights back on and began a slow, careful follow. The trip didn't take long. A mile away, the man parked his car in front of a very pleasant Spanish looking bungalow. Nothing ostentatious. Just tasteful and well cared for.

What's going on here? Who is Henry Blake in bed with?

January 28, 1926
Twenty-four Days AFTER the Harris Shooting
Saturday Evening at Gloria Swanson's

"Dressed to kill," Beatrice proudly announced to Walt that Saturday night when Rosie entered the living room, outfitted in a fashionable flapper dress. "I made her dress. Isn't it stylish?"

Made, hah. Killed herself to finish it on time was more like it. Rosie looked at her mother's calloused fingers and the inflamed thumb where she had accidentally jabbed herself with a straight pin. The dress, although lovely, also held a secret. Rosie knew the Chenille, the French lace, and the band fabric on the hat had undoubtedly all been covertly cut off from three different bolts of fabric in the costume room. She had confronted her mother about it at their first fitting.

"Mama, if you've stolen these fabrics, just think how much trouble you will be in if you get caught. You'll probably get fired."

With a pin still lodged in her lips, Beatrice had shrugged. She pushed it back into her wrist cushion and muttered, "It'd be worth it."

Now, smiling proudly, Beatrice said, "Take a picture of her, Walt."

He did. Two of them in fact. Rosie sat down. "Do you ever get these photographs developed?" she asked.

"Sure, at a friend's darkroom," Walt said.

Rosie laughed. "So, when are we gonna see them?

"They're home in my Hollywood collection."

Beatrice looked at her daughter. "That's because you're going to be a star, Rosie." She turned to Walt. "Right, Walt?"

Rosie couldn't remember the last time she had seen her mother this pumped up. It was disquieting. So much pressure. And just for a party?

Suddenly, the urge to have an animal cuddle was overwhelming. She gave a low whistle and was heartened to see Patches come bounding into the room. He immediately jumped up into her arms.

"Rosie, your dress!" Beatrice shrieked.

"Oh, Mama, it's not that important. It truly isn't."

Beatrice looked as though her daughter had just stabbed her with her sewing scissors. Immediately, Rosie led Patches away from the couch.

"Sorry, Mama." Rosie immediately felt guilty, as flashes of Johnny Paige having just left them sifted through her brain, along with her mother's sobs coming out of her parents' bedroom night after night. Even as a little girl she had tried to calm Beatrice down, but it had never worked. It still hadn't worked a year later, when a neighbor's dog had strayed into their backyard and dug up a single rose bush. Beatrice had let out a bloodcurdling scream then. Now, as a lesser version of that same kind of hysteria had just come from her mother, Rosie steeled herself for more.

She was relieved to see the passage of time had actually calmed her mother down. This time Beatrice pulled herself together quickly. "Overtired, I guess," she said simply.

When the producer's car horn tooted outside, Rosie got her wrap and stood in place as she touched her hat and quickly smoothed down her dress.

"Rosie?" Walt asked. "What are you doing?"

"I'm waiting for the limo driver to come. I think we all know Mr. Berns isn't going to come to the door." Sure enough, a strong knock came next, and opening up the door to the same driver, he stood there, stiff and impeccable in his uniform. He gave a short head jerk indicating they should go.

"Goodnight, Rosey-Posey," Walt said behind her.

Beatrice hugged her. "Make me proud." After she kissed her daughter's cheek, she stood watching her girl disappear into the dark car. From the back seat, Rosie noticed this time there were no waves from her mother, just a quick about-turn into their courtyard.

No matter how little Hollywood impressed her, no matter how annoyed she could get at her mother's longing to be up close and personal with movie stars, when Rosie saw Gloria Swanson's mansion, it literally took her breath away. In spite of herself, she gasped.

"Oh, my."

"Yes, it is quite impressive, isn't it?" Berns straightened his bowtie. "Definitely swanky."

Finally, he speaks, Rosie thought dryly. For some reason their trip over had been quite different from the first time he had taken her out. Her several attempts at polite conversation had fallen flat. He just didn't reply. Instead, he chose to bury his head in some paperwork the entire time.

From the curb, she could see two narrow concrete pathways encircling a large pond. Bulrushes interspersed with flat, green lily pads, where frogs placidly sat. In the murky water below, massive orange koi fish darted in and out and side to side.

Beyond the pond lay the house itself. A two-story high stucco structure with light brown tiles, it housed two cupolas on either side. Rounded awnings hovered over the tall Mediterranean style windows and over the grand front entrance double doors. Strolling up one of the pathways, Berns became almost chatty.

"Apparently, those koi fish were imported from Japan. At five hundred bucks each, they have grown into beauties, don't you agree?"

"Yes," Rosie said absently. She suddenly thought of hugging and petting Patches and Ginger. *Can't do that with a fish.*

In front of the house, a lone security guard stood at the main door as people were filing in. Soon, she and Berns were also inside the two-story high, echo-laden foyer with a wide double staircase on either side of the room. Ornate wrought iron bannisters swooped down along the two staircases, like graceful waves in the Pacific Ocean.

Stunning evening gowns, black coat tails, long-stringed pearls, and feathered headdresses were everywhere. Cigarettes jutted out from their slender dark holders, as a few guests actually glanced in her direction. Soon, it became obvious why. It was because of her escort.

"Good to see you, Berns," a cultured sounding gentleman with a British accent said.

"Dahling, is this your newest?" a middle-aged femme fatale asked, with a long drawl. She gave Rosie a good up-and-down stare.

"Not bad, not bad, Berns," added a young mustached man with slicked back hair.

Nodding, Berns seemed to take everything in his stride. He guided Rosie into the massive living room, where the din was pitched at a full roar. She was beginning to feel faint.

Eddie, how I wish you were here. She paused. *No, I don't because maybe you're not who I thought you were.*

Tired of her own mental ruminations, she looked around. Charlie Chaplin was across the room, tossing his head back in a burst of laughter. Next to him stood Douglas Fairbanks and Harold Lloyd. *Oh, my, wouldn't Mama just love all this!*

When Berns started conversing with an elegantly dressed woman, balancing a long, diamond-studded cigarette holder between her fingers, Rosie waited for the producer to introduce her. But he never did, and growing bored, her eyes swept across the crowd once more. She settled on a familiar looking heavy-set man next to the buffet table, helping himself to vast quantities of food.

"Why, that's what's-his-name," she said softly.

Berns followed the focus of her gaze. "Fatty Arbuckle. What the devil is he doing here?" He sounded annoyed.

"Oh, let the man enjoy himself, Bernsie. He's already been treated so badly by the film industry. He and Gloria go way back, you know."

The voice was feminine, yet deep and throaty. Turning around, Rosie faced the speaker. The woman was pleasant looking enough, but her outfit was spectacularly outlandish. Her headdress was pope-like in shape, dramatic in ornamentation. On it, little tiny diamonds lay in circles of dots. Her dress was accessorized by a floor-length green and blue floral kimono and her neck choker was black velvet, with a stunning emerald brooch.

The amazing creature stepped in closer. "Hello, dear. My name is Alla Nazimova. And yours is?"

"Rosie Paige."

"Welcome, Rosie Paige." Alla extended her hand, and when Rosie took it, the woman's grip seemed to last forever, with no signs of letting go. Rosie could feel her face flush as she tried to extricate herself from the aggressive woman.

Finally, she managed to break free.

Alla chortled. "So, you're Bernsie's new find, hmm? I'd love to invite you to one of my 'Sewing Circles.'"

Berns shook his head. "Give the girl a break, Alla. All in good time, all in good time. Well, nice chatting with you. Rosie, my dear, let's move on."

"Sewing circle?" Rosie asked as soon as they were at the buffet table.

He paused. "Frankly, it has nothing to do with sewing." Chuckling, he held up a plate. "Food? A drink?"

She shook her head. "Well, what does it have to do with then?"

He pointed to a corner across the room, near where they had just been. There was Alla, her arm around a woman's shoulder, squeezing her tightly. Suddenly, she ardently kissed the woman on the mouth.

"Oh, dear," Rosie muttered and looked up at the producer.

His eyes didn't quite match his smile. "Welcome to Hollywood."

When cheers and applause burst forth from the foyer, he placed her arm through his and moved them back into the front room. Like a well-choreographed burlesque show, everyone there was turning in tandem to look upward. A hush fell over the crowd, and with the exception of Charlie Chaplin's laughter ringing through from the living room, all the guests around Rosie and Berns seemed suspended in time.

A vision in white stood at the top of the stairs. Like milky droplets of dew, dozens of pearls adorned the woman's satin bodice, a bodice where the dangerously plunging neckline and sleeveless straps began, and from her waist, a long flowing satin skirt continued. Chiffon served as a delicate shawl, lightly covering some of her luscious skin. Yet Rosie's eyes did not rest long on the regal gown. She was riveted on what lay atop of the movie star's head. A white-feathered headdress expanded a good yard high and two feet out. Trailing across her brow were more pearls, strung in a delicate pattern that coated her forehead and settled down around her eyes.

Gloria Swanson was making her grand entrance. Down the wide staircase she floated, her intense eyes sparkling down at her audience, her lips poised in a radiant smile. As soon as she made it to the floor, she was instantly cocooned in a tight circle of guests, who kissed her cheeks and patted her back.

"Thank you all for coming," she announced gaily. "Oh, Mr. DeMille, remember in my very first movie, when you insisted I let a lion lie on my back?"

Laughter exploded all around as Rosie strained to see the famous film director. But the crowd had moved on with the celebrity into the living room, and Rosie could feel herself and Berns being swept along with them.

Inside the all-white living room, Rosie tugged on Bern's jacket sleeve. "Lion on top of her?"

The producer looked at her horrified expression. "Rosie, if you want to succeed in this business, sometimes you have to do things you don't want to do." His eyes narrowed. "Now, how about that drink?"

She nodded this time. *I could sure use one.* He produced a flask and handed it over, smirking as she guzzled down several swallows. On an empty stomach, her head quickly started to reel as Berns signaled someone over. It was the corpulent man she had seen at the Brown Derby, sitting at a nearby table with a young woman.

"Rosie, this is Floyd Hutchins, agent to the stars. I have some connections to make, so I'll leave you in his capable hands. See you soon."

"But—" She began to sway sideways, in an effort to avoid the smoke coming from Hutchins' thick cigar. Up close he was even more repulsive than he had looked from a distance at the Brown Derby.

"So, honey, you want to be a star, huh? Well, Berns and I can take you there."

Just then a slim, nervous looking young man in a tuxedo walked by them. He nodded politely to Rosie, but gave only a curt nod to Hutchins.

"You see that fellow? He's the darling of the studios. Irving Thalberg is his name. They call him the Wonder Boy."

"I don't know him," she said, feeling dizzier by the minute.

"Sweetie, all I can say is if you get in with him, then you're golden. Something we can work on together, hmm?"

Rosie cringed. *I don't belong here.*

He slung his arm around her shoulders. "And to think I'll only take five percent. Most agents take double that, you know."

Suddenly, the room erupted into applause. A tango had begun, and Gloria announced loudly, "Rudy, darling, they're playing our song!"

The crowd edged backward toward the walls to reveal Gloria and the most famous Hollywood leading man in the world—Rudolph Valentino.

"Oh, my. He's the reason why my mother wanted to come to Hollywood," Rosie said.

When Hutchins looked down at her with a smirk, the deadness of his eyes gave her a sudden chill.

Swanson and Valentino were magnificent—their timing impeccable—as they walked forward and back, their eyes locked in a passionate gaze, their arms posed in a Spanish Flamenco-like hold. All eyes were on the dancers themselves. But as the music swelled, Rosie couldn't stop looking at their footwork—Gloria, twisting sexily around him in heels; Valentino, stepping in and out between her legs in his pointed-toed boots. No wonder he had become an overnight success after people saw him in *The Four Horsemen of the Apocalypse!*

The music ended and after an exaggerated bow, first to Swanson, then to the delighted crowd, Valentino kissed her hand and left, a roar of applause following him out.

Immediately, Rosie could hear women screaming, as police sirens blared.

"Let's go see what's going on, honey," Hutchins said. He grabbed Rosie's hand, and let them both be swallowed up by all the guests' scramble to get out the front door.

Outside, it was sheer pandemonium. Hordes of women had pushed past the security guard and clustered around Valentino. Sobbing, stretching out their arms to him, some of them held up his headshot photograph for autographs. They were relentless.

Looking through hats and female bodies, Rosie caught a glimpse of the star. His smile, so charming before, had been replaced by pressed lips and eyes filled with cold fear. She had heard tales about his crazy fans, but seeing their frenzied state was truly frightening.

Sirens continued to wail as more and more police cars arrived and policemen rushed onto the scene.

Barking orders of "Stand back," "Leave him be," and "Get him out of here," interfused with women wailing, "Valentino, marry me," and "You're my one true love."

The crowd became a ground swell—moving to the right, then to the left, as Valentino was plucked from his followers and quickly helped into one of the police paddy wagons.

Deprived of "their Rudy," the women grew desperate. En masse the mob tried to pursue the wagon, and in doing so, people were being knocked to the ground.

Rosie was one of them. Stunned at first, at ground level she was unable to see anything but women's skirts and shoes, stepping over her and knocking into her side.

Eddie. Oh, God, if only you were here. Her mind swirled. Finally, she shouted, "Help!"

Suddenly, she was yanked up to a standing position as the rest of the women were either running toward the street or being muscled into police wagons. Catching her breath, she looked up at her rescuers—Berns and Hutchins.

"Thank God," she muttered.

"Sorry about that, Rosie, my dear," Berns said coolly. "Hazards of stardom." He put his arm around her shoulders. "Listen, I've got to meet up with the head of Medford inside. Hutchins will take you home." He looked over at the bulky man, chomping on his cigar. "Right, Floyd? She lives at the Highland Courts."

"Sure. Come on, Rosie, I'll take you home." He winked at Berns.

Hutchins pointed to his car parked nearby. "My brand new 1926 Renault CV NM is at your service," he said proudly as he helped her in.

Obviously, this was his pride and joy. Still, she was too tired and wobbly to do anything but nod. Settled in the front, she vaguely wondered why Hutchins had given Berns a wink, but quickly pushed that thought aside.

She could hear a trolley car clanging nearby as they made their way toward Hollywood. Aware of his continuous glances toward her as he drove, her mind raced. *Just get me home, just get me home.*

"Hey, Rosie girl, why don't you snuggle closer to me?" he said after a while, breaking her silence.

Her head whipped around toward him. "Are you joking?" she blurted out.

He grinned. "I'd never joke about something like that."

"Like what?" Her voice strong before, now held a quaver. With his left hand still on the wheel, he tried to pull her over toward him with his right.

"Scoot on over, honey," he said, his foul cigar breath wafting into her face. She shoved him back.

His eyes bulging slightly, he steered over to the curb and stopped the car. "Dammit, I said scoot on over."

He reached out for her with both hands and jerked her close. Again, she shoved him back. Growling, he leaned over and grabbed by her throat. "You'll do what I say or else, you little bitch!"

Startled, she struggled to get to her door handle, but he was stronger. He crushed her against him and grappled with her dress. The harder she fought, the more determined he grew. She could feel her dress being ripped, and suddenly, she thought of all her mother's hard work to make it. That gave her an extra shot of adrenaline. She reached up and as hard as she could, palm-butted his nose.

Yelping with pain, he let her go for a few seconds. That was her chance. She tugged on her door handle, and the door flew open. She tumbled out of the car and onto the ground.

"You bitch, you little bitch," he hollered. She could hear his car door open, the heavy clomp of his shoes coming around to her.

Like a shot, she was up and running. Panic made her fly down the street, aware of Hutchins behind her by his belabored breathing. Faster and faster she ran, not even stopping when she could no longer hear Hutchins, just the night sounds of an owl and a trolley finishing its last run.

I can't go home, I just can't. Eddie. I need Eddie. She leaned against a building, struggling to catch her breath. *I don't care if you're guilty.*

Eddie had just turned out his light when Mabel banged on his door. He blew out his cheeks. *Another phone call from God knows who?*

"Eddie, Eddie! Rosie's here," his landlady said in a loud stage whisper.

In a flash, he was at the door. There she was, standing beside Mabel. Her face was glistening with sweat and tears, her hair every which way, and her dress, torn down the middle. Sobbing, she collapsed into his arms. Over her head, he looked at a wide-eyed Mabel who shrugged then disappeared down the hall.

"Rosie, Rosie," he coaxed gently, trying not to show his horror. "Come sit down with me and tell me what happened." He maneuvered her over to his bed and slowly sat down with her. Hyperventilating, she tried to talk but only loud, gulping noises were coming out of her mouth. He started to stroke and rub her back in a slow, steady rhythm, and after a couple of minutes, he could feel her body relax, her sobs soften into weak mews.

"It was Hutchins," she said.

His "Who is Hutchins?" came out like a low growl.

"A famous agent, Berns told me."

"Never heard of him," he said calmly enough. *I'm gonna kill this guy.* Her head on his chest, he could feel her exhaustion now, and when he lifted her face up to him, her dried tears had left two streaks of mascara down her cheeks.

"Oh, Eddie," she said simply.

"Sleep, Rosie, just sleep. You're safe now. I'll call your mama, and let her know you're here."

She nodded, crying softly. "I hate this town, Eddie, I truly do."

"Get some rest," he said, his eyes moistening.

"Will you lie down with me?" she whispered.

Together they sank down on the Murphy bed. He pulled a blanket over them and wrapped his arms around her. Even with all of this happening, he marveled at how well their bodies fit together, and soon, he was relieved to hear her gentle breathing.

"Rosie, still awake?" There was a pause.

"Yes, barely," she murmured.

"I just want to tell you something," he said, snuggling tighter against her.

"Uh-huh. What?" Her voice sounded heavy, more than ready to escape into unconsciousness.

He could tell she was drifting off. "You weren't put on this earth to fix your mama's woes, you know. You have a right to be happy."

"Thank you, Eddie," she whispered. Then she was sound asleep. He waited a while longer, then, quietly extracted himself from her, rose from the bed, walked down the hall to the phone, and dialed.

"Hello Mrs. Paige? It's Eddie," he said into the mouthpiece.

"Eddie?" Rosie's not here," Beatrice said on the other end. Her familiar sour voice was ever present.

"I know. She's here with me. She's all right, but there was an incident tonight, and she was very upset. She's sleeping now, but I promise to bring her back in the morning."

"What happened?" Beatrice's voice exploded into the phone.

"It's a long story. I'll let her tell you. But the main thing is, she's all right, Mrs. Paige, I promise. See you tomorrow morning." Click. He hung up, not waiting to hear what she had to say.

Back in his room, he made sure Rosie was fully covered, then sat down in his chair across from her. As she slept, he studied her face, so angelic in its peacefulness. Her curls lay crusted onto her cheeks, and her lips were formed into a gentle, dreamlike smile.

He could feel his heart ache with protectiveness.

"Sleep, Rosie," he said into the quiet room. "And don't worry. I'll still be here when you figure it all out."

CHAPTER THIRTEEN

"I never said, 'I want to be alone.' I only said, 'I want to be left alone!' There is all the difference."
— Greta Garbo, actress

January 28, 1926
Twenty-four Days AFTER the Harris Shooting
That Same Night

BEATRICE WAS FUMING. How *dare* Eddie think he knew what Rosie's needs were! How like a man, to take over whenever he felt like it. Flashbacks of her husband, Johnny, exploded in her brain. How smug he had been the morning he left, telling her how boring she was and how he wanted much more out of life than she could ever offer.

Still sputtering, she dialed Walt up to tell him the disturbing news. To her dismay, when he picked up the phone, he sounded more than a little fuzzy. *Oh dear, he's been drinking a lot recently.* Worry straddled there between Rosie's troubles and Walt's drinking. He was, after all, their Rock of Gibraltar.

"Walt, it's about Rosie. Please come over as soon as you can. I need you." She fought back tears.

"Is she all right?" His voice instantly sounded tense.

"I'll explain when you get here."

"I'm on my way," he said. Before he hung up, she could hear him hacking and coughing.

She began to pace up and down the hallway then spilled out into the living room. *What went wrong? Rosie was with Berns, at a respectable party, for goodness sake, not a party at Clara Bow's den of iniquity.* Beatrice could feel the bile rise up into her throat and spin into her thoughts. Just goes to show, no man could be trusted. They'd always let you down. And why did Rosie run to Eddie instead of coming home? Didn't she realize her mother was the only one who was truly looking after her? Well, Walt, too. Didn't she know that she could count on the both of them to be her true supporters? Certainly not Eddie.

Her chest tightened like a vise, she continued to circle the living room, muttering to herself. At one point, she clasped her hands together. They felt clammy.

As angry as she had been with Detective Lozano, the idea of contacting him was growing on her. He would know how to handle the situation. Break down Eddie's door and arrest him if need be. After all, Rosie had told her that the detective had admitted Eddie was the main suspect in the recent killings. If the law came down on him again, that "golden boy" wouldn't dare defy it.

She heard the front door's lock open with a click. *Walt, thank God!* Instantly, she ran over to him and flung her arms around his neck, her tears coming in fast.

After several murmurs of "It's gonna be okay," he stepped back. "Now, tell me, what in the world happened? Is Rosie here?"

Beatrice shook her head and led him over to the sofa. Together, they sank down into the pillows.

"She's at Eddie's."

"What? I thought she didn't want to see him."

"Eddie called me to say Rosie was there, sleeping. All's he said was there had been an incident, but she should be the one to tell us. He also said he would bring her back in the morning.

"Do you trust him to keep his word?" Walt asked.

"I don't know. So, we're gonna call that Detective Lozano. He gave Rosie his home number. I'll get it now."

"The one who got Rosie drunk?"

"Yes, but according to Rosie, he's questioned Eddie several times in connection with the Harris murder. Because the detective is familiar with the case, he'll know how to get under Eddie's skin. He'll force him to let her go."

"I don't know, Bea. It's kind of late. Besides, maybe we shouldn't get too involved with that detective."

Ignoring him, she sprang up and went into Rosie's room to get the number. When she made the call, Walt stayed on the couch, his head in his hands. Twenty minutes later, Lozano's loud double pound on the front door sounded like a bass drum. As soon as she explained the situation, the three of them were in Frank's car, speeding over to Eddie's—Beatrice in front, biting her nails, Walt in back, sneaking in gin.

Frank saw Mabel's immediate scowl the minute she opened up to him.

"What the hell? What are you doing here again, detective? And who are these folks?"

Her bathrobe, obviously laundered multiple times had, in certain spots, become threadbare, close to transparent. With a head full of curlers and her nightly slather of cold cream all over her face, the landlady almost had a comical look to her. But no one was laughing.

"We're here for Miss Paige," Frank said. He leaned in and gave his most threatening look.

Mabel didn't bat an eye. She held up her palm. "Hold it, buster."

Frank pushed his badge into her face. "Police business. Got it?"

"You think that makes a difference?" she muttered. Still, she made a "follow me" gesture with her hand and led them down the hall to Eddie's room.

What a crazy broad. As they walked, Frank watched her bathrobe in front of him swish back and forth, her slippers scraping and sliding against the floorboards.

Just outside Eddie's door, Mabel turned to the group and hissed, "Sssh, be quiet. Rosie's sleeping." She leaned in toward the three of them. "Peacefully," she added, her nostrils flaring.

She knocked softly.

Immediately, they heard shuffling behind the door. Eddie opened it up no more than a foot. Taking in the entourage, he shook his head.

"Why are you here? I told you she's sleeping," he said to Beatrice.

Huffing, she shoved past him and strode into the room, then stopped.

Rosie couldn't have looked more peaceful. A dark blue blanket lay nestled up around her chin. Her head, indented into Eddie's downy pillow, looked like a little curly-haired girl, encased by soft peaks and valleys of white.

"See? She's safe and sound, Mrs. Paige," Eddie said quietly and pressed a finger to his lips. "Let's not wake her up."

Frank stared at the perfect picture of innocence. *Damn, she does look safe and sound.*

"Yes, she does look peaceful," Beatrice murmured, her eyes misty.

"You know, I would never let Rosie come to any harm," Eddie said in a low voice to both Frank and Beatrice. "And, as promised, I will bring her over to you tomorrow. Just name the time."

"We'll come pick her up. Just call us when she wakes up," Beatrice said. "Right, Walt?"

Eddie nodded as Frank casually glanced over at Walt who was standing by the bureau, staring at the photos sitting on top of it.

"Walt, did you hear me?" she asked.

He paused a couple of seconds. "Sure," he said absently and walked back to her.

Curious, Frank stepped over to the photos. Just different strangers, he thought. He leaned in closer. A photo of Eddie with Lon Chaney stared back at him. Shrugging, he turned around and joined Beatrice and Walt at the door. After they left, he started to follow them, but at the last minute, swung around and leaned back into the room.

"Willis, this doesn't mean you're off the hook, you know. You're still our number one suspect in the Harris case."

His head cocked to one side, Eddie narrowed his eyes. "Just go."

Frank dished out a smug wink before he left. But walking down the hall, he sighed. Trouble was, he was having a hard time believing his own words.

The next morning, after a fine breakfast in bed—provided by Mabel—Rosie looked a lot better.

"Eddie, I can't stand this town," she said. "I've been doing some thinking." She started to sniffle again. "I'm going to tell Mama I want out of Hollywood. That the only thing that makes me happy is being with animals. Certainly not being a big star."

"Look, Rosie, I'm really glad you came to this decision, but right now I've gotta call your mother and tell her it's okay for her and Walt to pick you up.

Why don't you get dressed? Mabel has given me one of the dresses left behind by a former tenant. Here it is."

After he handed her a lightweight, unattractive dress, he drew her into his arms for a long, tender hug and a soft kiss on her cheek.

"It'll all work out, Rosie," he murmured. "You know you got my support no matter what you do."

Within the hour, they could hear Beatrice and Walt come in the front door—Beatrice, with her sharp staccato clacks on the hall floor, Walt with a shuffle, and at one point, what sounded like a crash against the wall.

"Oh, dear," Rosie said, exchanging looks with Eddie.

"Yeah."

When the two visitors entered, Eddie was shocked. Walt's face was crimson, his stance wobbly.

"Rosie, dear, ready to go?" Beatrice asked as she stroked her daughter's arm. "Walt told me he has to go to an appointment soon, so we need to hurry."

Eddie watched Walt place a hand on the front of his dresser—slowly, self-consciously. *He's blotto!*

"Look, why don't I take you and Rosie home, Mrs. Paige," he said. "That way Walt can go directly on to his appointment."

"I'm gonna take the girls home," Walt said, his voice low-pitched.

One of Eddie's cheek muscles twitched. "Mrs. Paige, I really urge you to let me take you both home."

"This is my family, Willis, not yours!" Walt's eyes flashed.

Beatrice looked from one man to the other. Then, placing her hand on Walt's arm, she said, "Walt, dear, I think it would be best if Eddie took us home, after all. You've got somewhere to go, and I wouldn't want to hold you up."

A low grunt came out of him.

"Listen," she said, "Of *course*, we're your family. But right now, you go on to your appointment. We'll expect you for breakfast tomorrow."

His bloodshot eyes stared down at her.

Beatrice smiled. "I'll walk you out. Just know, we'd be nothing without you."

As she guided Walt out, Eddie and Rosie nodded their thanks.

Something was different at the police station. Frank could just feel it. People were bustling about, minding their "P's and Q's." Still, he sensed something was up. He was right. No sooner had he risen to go refresh his coffee, then Captain Billings hand-signaled him into his office. *Oh, so we're pals again?* Frank made his way over to him with a certain degree of skepticism. Passing the interrogation room, he noticed one of their chief interrogators talking to a red-faced man with jerky hand movements and wild-looking eyes. A few hairs immediately stood up in formation on the back of his neck. *Uh-oh.*

"Yes, captain?" he asked as he poked his head inside his boss' office door.

"Go to the interrogation room right now. It looks like we've nabbed the killer," Billings said smugly.

"Of the Harris case?" Frank could feel his heartbeat doing flip-flops.

"Naw, I doubt it. But certainly, the other killing a few Sunday nights ago."

Upon entering the small room, Frank almost gagged. The stench was so powerful, the interrogator was holding a handkerchief up to his nose, his eyes watery.

"Lozano, this here is Bobby Starr. Ain't you, Bobby?" the interrogator said.

The putrid smelling man grinned. "Yeah, last time I checked." When he opened his mouth, Frank nearly threw up. The room reeked of male sweat and overwhelming halitosis.

"Tell Detective Lozano what you just told me."

Starr drew himself up. "I copied him, is all. I've always wanted to bump someone off, so I got me a rifle, so I could copy him."

"Who?" Frank asked, needing to hear the man actually say it.

"The Harris killer. Read about him in all the papers. I sure liked what he did."

Staying as far away from Starr as possible, Frank asked, "Why, for God's sake?"

"Because he did it from a rooftop. He got good aim. He's my hero."

The interrogator leaned back in his chair. "Did you dislike Harris the producer? You know, the victim?" he asked.

Bobby looked confused. "How do I know? Never saw Harris before in my life."

"What about Mark Oliver or Willy Sweet?" Frank added. "They were also shot with a rifle."

"Who? Never heard of any of 'em." Bobby let out a belch, sending another wave of stink throughout the room.

Shaking his head, the interrogator clamped cuffs hard over Bobby Starr's wrists. "Well, one down at least," he said, as he shoved the prisoner off to the south end of the station, accompanied by various hoots and applause.

Back at his desk, Frank tried to concentrate on the three manila folders stacked in front of him. The top one was marked "Chester Harris." But it was the other two beneath it that he was once again revisiting. Unlike the Harris case, these older folders were crumbling at their corners, and their ink, instead of black like the more recent case, had, over time, become a sienna brown.

He took out one labeled, "Mark Oliver," opened it up, and restudied its contents. A photograph of a pleasant looking young man faced upward at him. Twenty-five years old, an unsuccessful clerk, somewhere. A nobody, really. *Wait a minute. He did live in a known mob area.*

Frank's pulse picked up a notch.

Next, he went for the folder underneath that, labeled: "Willy Sweet." Worked as a RKO mechanic. *Hmm. Both he and Harris worked in the film business. Wonder if they knew each other? If so, was there also a mob connection?*

He shook his head. Maybe these guys were done in by the mob, but with no leads, what could he do? A feeling of hopelessness washed over him just as Shire plunked down on his desk chair.

"Lozano, give it up," his partner said and reached for his bottom drawer handle.

Frank knew exactly what he was looking for. "Shire, we now have three unsolved rifle shot murders on our hands, in a span of what—two years? That ain't good, and you know it." He continued to watch Shire glance around quickly before handing his flask over to his partner.

Frank snatched it up, and bending down in front of his desk, took two fast swigs, then covertly returned it to Shire.

"You tried, God knows," Shire said. "Maybe these guys were involved in mob hits. Maybe they were in the wrong place at the wrong time. Or maybe, it was just their time. Let it go, Frank."

"Yeah, I know. According to Billings, these other two dead men were considered low priority, unlike the Big Cheese producer, Harris. And all's we've got for *his* case is peanuts."

"What about that Willis guy? I thought you all were so ready to finger him," Shire said.

"Yeah, he's still a suspect." Frank suddenly got busy organizing the files again, not looking at his partner.

Shire nodded his head slowly. "I thought so. More politics." His eyes slit. "Remember that case years ago, the one where the whole family was killed? What is it you said to me then about this job?"

Frank looked up, his sigh long-drawn. "It's enough to destroy a man's soul."

After completely crashing the moment she returned from Eddie's, Rosie didn't wake up until four o'clock in the afternoon. When she finally entered the kitchen, Walt was busy reading the newspaper and showing no signs of his behavior from that morning. Beatrice was planted next to him, calmly studying a new McCall's dress pattern.

Good. For now, everyone's nice and peaceful. Maybe when she told them her feelings there wouldn't be the usual dramatics. What happened with Hutchins was enough to last her quite a while, thank you very much.

Walt looked up at her, and pointed to the latest headline. "Lookee here. They're calling this man they just arrested, Bobby Starr, the copycat killer."

"What do you mean copycat?" Beatrice asked.

"Seems this man wanted to be exactly like the Harris killer." Walt shook his head.

Rosie came over to the breakfast nook and sat down opposite them. Her head pounding, she wondered if this was a good time to say what she had made up her mind to say. Probably not quite yet. She watched the two of them, so immersed in their different interests—shoulders touching, Walt reading parts aloud, other times silently. Still, she knew her mother. Secretly she was probably waiting with baited breath to find out what happened after Gloria's party.

Sure enough, Beatrice soon started in. "So. Are you ready to tell us what happened?"

Walt looked up as well, his eyes slightly glazed over, his lips etched in a tight pucker.

"Berns is not who you think he is, Mama. At the party, he abandoned me to this agent, this horror of a man, who basically attacked me on the way home."

"What?" both exclaimed.

"It's a long story, but I managed to escape from him."

"To Eddie's," Walt said quietly.

"Yes, why not us?" Beatrice asked. "Why Eddie's for goodness sake?"

"Mama, you have to stop this about him. He's a good man."

"You told me he's a suspect in the Harris case. Besides, he reminds me of your father."

"Because he looks like Papa? Oh, Mama."

Suddenly, the kitchen wall clock's light *tick-tick-tick* sounded more like *boom-boom-boom*.

Rosie shifted in her seat. *Do I dare tell them my feelings now?*

Unknowingly, Beatrice did it for her. "Rosie, I know you. You have something else on your mind."

Walt put down the paper and stared at her.

Rosie drew a deep breath. "You know me too well, Mama. Yes, I do have something else on my mind."

Beatrice started drumming her fingers on the tabletop as fast as any hot jazz musician.

They were both poised and waiting. It was now or never. Rosie blinked several times then jumped in. "I don't want this Hollywood life anymore." She paused long enough for that to sink in. "Look, Mama, the fact is I never wanted it. I only did it because you wanted me to."

The stunned silence was so palpable, Patches trotted over with a watery gaze in his eyes. He jumped up on Rosie's lap and licked her face.

"Put that dog down, for goodness sakes," Beatrice snapped.

Rosie started to comply, then stopped. "No. This is what makes me happy, Mama."

"What, a dog jumping on your lap?"

"Yes, exactly that. You know I have always loved animals. Not movies or that world."

"What would you do instead?" She could feel Walt's eyes on her.

"Dr. Peterson, the veterinarian, told me he would be willing to hire me."

"But...but..." Beatrice stammered.

"He also told me he could put in a good word for me in other towns or cities if I ever wanted to move away."

Beatrice's eyes moistened. "Why would he even say that?"

"Because I told him how unhappy I was in this 'glamour town.'"

"So, basically, you are going to leave your mother?" Walt asked slowly.

"Oh, Walt, who knows? I've just realized all of this."

She reached out for her mother's hand. "Sorry, Mama. If I do go, you could come with me. I know how exhausting it's been for you, sewing costumes for actors and actresses who get paid so much more money than you, it's a joke."

Tic-tic-tic the clock sounded.

Beatrice exploded. "It's Eddie, isn't it? He's from up north, from that little nothing town. He put you up to this!"

"Goodness, no! I only just told him about all this."

Tic-tic-tic.

Walt suddenly reached into his jacket pocket and pulled out his flask.

"Walt—" Beatrice began, but he ignored her. He opened it up and took several gulps.

"Rosie, look what you've made Walt do." Beatrice's eyes were filling up with tears.

Tick-tick-tick.

"Just think of all the wonderful sights and the fine things you have around here, Rosie-Posey," Walt said. "As a matter of fact, I was finally going to show you both my Hollywood collection."

Rosie stared at him. "My lord, Walt, you've been talking about that room for over a year, and you've never showed us. Why now?"

He took another slug of gin. "Seeing as you're leaving the business and maybe Los Angeles, I think it's time to show my favorite gals my room."

"Your collection? Oh, my," Beatrice wiped her eyes. She turned to Rosie. "See what you'd be missing if you moved?"

Rosie smiled at her mother. "Oh, Mama. I do love you." To Walt, she said, "So when are we going to see your famous exhibit?"

For several seconds, he seemed deep in thought. "How about this coming Saturday evening?"

"Goody-goody!" Beatrice clapped her hands.

Smiling, Rosie was relieved to see peace being restored, after all. "Yes, goody-goody. I'll be there for sure."

"No date with Eddie?" Walt asked.

"No, sir, you shall have my full attention." Her little salute sparked a smile from her mother.

"Then, ladies, it's a date," he said.

January 4, 1926
The Morning of the Harris Shooting and the Start of It All

The last notice about his target had come. The scheduled time was specified, and the outdoor Medford set with Harris on it, a certainty. Earlier that morning, Alonzo Casale figured he should have a bit of breakfast, but not too much. After all, this was his first time "on deck." He sure didn't want to feel nauseous as he squeezed the trigger. A nice piece of toast with jam on it and a cup of tea to steady his nerves seemed to work well, as he studied a photograph of Harris once again, for the hundredth time.

He checked the expensive watch his cousin Tony had given him for the shooting.

"I want you to have the exact time, kid, not from some cheap crap you'd get off the streets," he had told Alonzo two days before. With his arm around his younger cousin, his pride and support were reassuring.

By nine o'clock, Alonzo knew it was time to go. He quickly made the sign of the cross, picked up his rifle bag, and headed out, destiny staring him in the face.

CHAPTER FOURTEEN

"Those who never make mistakes lose a great many chances to learn something."
— Mary Pickford, actress

February 3, 1926
Thirty Days AFTER the Harris Shooting
The Following Week, Friday Afternoon

FRANK LOOKED UP, spied the two expensively dressed men retreating into Billing's office with the captain and expelled a harsh breath. *Crawford here again? And who the hell is that other guy with him? Probably Parrot. That can't be good.* He turned to Spire, who was also staring at the two dandies.

"That 'good time' Charlie Crawford's easy to recognize—the flash from his diamond rings could light up a room. But the other guy is Kent Kane Parrot, right?" Frank asked his partner.

Shire nodded. "Oh, yeah. That's him, all right."

"Parrot, what a stupid name. Never actually seen him before." Frank snorted.

"Yeah, well, that 'parrot,' along with Crawford, are responsible for getting our crooked, puppet mayor George Cryer elected."

Frank met his partner's eyes and sighed. *Enough said.* He glanced over at Shire's desk.

"What you working on?" Frank asked.

Shire shrugged. "You can complain all you want about Billings, but at least he's got you on better cases than what he gives me."

"Yeah, like what kind of cases?"

"Like some farmers out in the San Fernando Valley complaining they keep hearing rifle shots being fired in their orange groves on the weekends when their workers ain't there. They tell me they believe it's from a shooting club called the Buccaneers that sponsors this kinda thing. They even got membership numbers and sign in vouchers each time they go. And all without any of the farmers' permission. So, you see? You still get the Harris murder case—more or less—and I get the hayseed cases that nobody gives a damn about."

"The Buccaneers, huh? Be careful. Sounds like a bunch of nuts. About now, maybe I'd like to trade places with you." Frank noticed an impatient hand signal coming from Billings. The better-snap-to-his-office-immediately sort of signal. "So sick of being Billing's lapdog," he muttered.

Inside the captain's lair, the two visitors were busying chomping on Havana cigars, swilling down illegal hooch, and regaling each other with bawdy jokes. Sure enough, through the dim, smoked-filled room, Frank noticed how Crawford's diamond rings acted as a guiding light to his fashionable pinstriped suit, prominent bowtie, and his one wing-tipped shoe up and crossed over his other leg.

"You needed to see me, captain?"

The two men casually glanced over at Frank and chortled.

He could feel his blood pressure rise as he tried to ignore them. He knew the next words coming from Billing's mouth probably weren't going to be pretty.

They weren't.

"Look, Lozano, it's come to my attention, you've been going down a different path in the Harris case than the one we had agreed upon."

"Pardon?" Frank could feel his pulse surge.

"Why isn't this Eddie Willis fellow behind bars by now for both murders, detective?"

He could tell Billings was showing off for his guests. He was leaning back in his chair, his hands cupped behind his head, his chest expanded outward a good inch or two.

"For one thing," Frank said, "he had that alibi for the Sunday night murder. Remember? You were there with Willis, Lon Chaney, and a couple of lawyers."

Instantly, he realized his mistake. *Damn!* Not only did he indicate he had listened in on the Chaney and lawyer meeting, his snide tone had made Billings look foolish in front of his corrupt affiliates. *Oh, boy.* He was right. Billing's pink face spoke volumes.

"Enough of your crap, Lozano. Stick with the plan and no more questioning people you have no business dealing with."

In spite of himself, Frank blurted out, "You mean employees of the Iron Man?"

Another mistake. Now, Crawford's and Parrot's faces were shifting toward red. Angry red.

"You gonna get it through his head, Billings, or do we have to step in?" Parrot said, half rising out of his seat.

As Billing cleared his throat, Frank's stomach did a somersault. The captain was more bought and paid for than he had thought.

Drawing a shaky breath, he said to Billings directly. "I'll do what I can. What I always do, captain. Is that all?"

When Billings nodded curtly, Frank left, hearing behind him a snarl coming out of Parrot's mouth. "Get him in line, Billings. Or else."

Back at his desk, it took all of ten seconds for Frank to look over at his partner and comment, "I could sure drink something to get fried to the hat. You up for it?"

Shire chuckled. "Sure. These days I can always use a drink. Just don't telephone me later after you're drunk as a skunk, like the last time, okay? Didn't appreciate you waking me up."

As synchronized as the newly formed Rockettes out of New York City's Radio Music hall, the two detectives simultaneously placed their files to one side on their respective desks, grabbed their jackets slung over their chairs, and left the station.

By the time they walked into their standby, Smarty's, the place was crawling with bootleggers, working Joes, and floozies. For Frank, that was perfect. Downing one gin fizz after another, in short order he was soon beyond ossified and had some trouble seeing in front of him. Still, his sense of touch was intact. He could feel the big busted, low-cut flapper-gowned doll hanging onto his arm and giggling at every spoken word he uttered.

Shire had a gal, too, although his was very pretty with long, tantalizing gams. Frank's girl was less so, but it didn't really matter. If all went well, and where he was angling to go—on a bed in the dark—every dame had the same equipment.

Back in his apartment, he and his lady-for-the-night were both so hammered, they clung to each other as he tried to maneuver them both over to his bed. Once there, there were few sounds, save for the mutual grunts and "ouches" tossed out into the air as two sets of clothes were being ripped off and flung onto the floor. No tenderness, no long, deep kisses—just rutting, which suited them both just fine.

Until the morning, when Frank woke up with a banging headache and a sinking feeling in his gut as he stared down at the lipstick-smeared cheeks of the girl, all twisted up in his rumpled bed sheets. With a heavy sigh, he got up, located his strewn pants, yanked them on, and stumbled into his kitchen to brew up some coffee, the whole time recognizing his little tryst hadn't worked. His mind was still full of the corrupt Crawford and Parrot, Rosie and Eddie, and the unknown killer out there—scot-free.

February 4, 1926
Thirty-one Days AFTER the Harris Shooting
The Next Day, Saturday Morning

Heading to work on the trolley at seven-thirty in the morning, Beatrice settled back in her seat and let the car's movement lull her further into her thoughts. She had already had a very busy morning. Up at the crack of dawn, she had washed clothes and hung them out to dry, prepared Rosie's and her supper, and ironed Walt's shirts the way he liked them—crisp but not too heavy on the starch. There had been so many things to do. So many ways to keep her mind occupied so she could avoid facing a hard, cold fact—Rosie might very well leave her. And for that matter, leave Walt, too. It was bad enough her beautiful daughter wanted to abandon the seamstress's dreams of Hollywood stardom. But to give it all up to do what, work with animals? It was just too much to bear. And after all that she had done for Rosie. Bitterly, she flashed on how she had pleaded with the head of Medford's costume department to put in a good word for the girl with the casting director in exchange for Beatrice working extra-long shifts during the week and coming in on weekends. All those long, neck crimping hours, those finger pricks and backaches, and in the end, all for what? Nothing.

As automobiles honked and the trolley jiggled and clattered, visions of the countless nubile, clawing-their-way-to-the-top bit players came to mind—those girls who had come in for fittings these past two years, each one hungrier than the next for a chance to succeed. And always with a stream of chatter about their willingness to do whatever was necessary to get ahead in this star-studded Hollywood. Even now, remembering some of those confessions the girls had openly made to one another still made her blush.

Without warning, another thought popped up. *Wouldn't my Johnny have loved those girls.* She grimaced angrily. Startled by her sudden spark of rage after all this time, she recognized how unhealthy it was to dwell on the past, particularly seeing as how she could be facing a life without Rosie in the near future. It dawned on her that what she craved right now was to relax.

She closed her eyes, the clang of the trolley's bell reminding her she had only six more blocks to go before the exit in front of Medford Studios' huge gate. All too fast, *clang-clang* went the conductor's bell. As she rose from her seat, she instantly felt a stab of rheumatism in her right knee, coupled with a tiny spasm on the back of her neck. She shook her head. *If Rosie were to become a star with acres of money, we could get the best medical care in the world.*

"Medford stop. Medford, folks," the conductor announced. Instantly, she was surrounded by a cavalcade of suitcase-toting actors and actresses, carpenters, cameramen, cooks, and someone dressed in a full clown outfit, with a red bulbous nose and thick greasepaint, which featured black crosses highlighted over his eyes.

Stepping down from the trolley, she could feel herself drifting off into a fog of depression. Tears had formed and threatened to spill over when, without warning, she thought of Walt. *Wonder how he's doing? He seems so much calmer than me about all of this.* It seemed her moniker for him—the Rock of Gibraltar—certainly seemed to fit him.

Heartened by his strength, she smiled, and soon she could feel her mood lifting. So much so, inside the gate on her way to the costume department, she actually joked with Anna, one of her co-workers, who had caught up with her stride.

Outside the sewing room entrance, they were met by their boss, Mrs.

Latham, who was clearly upset. Her face looked pinched, her hands, twisted and clenched together.

"Thank goodness you're here, ladies. Mr. Harris' former assistant, Henry Blake, is coming in five minutes with a tall order. We have to finish that elaborate gown today for that actress, Mildred."

Anna chuckled. "You mean the skinny one with a double set of stars in her eyes?"

"Yes, now, let's get a move on, ladies." The head of costuming clapped her hands twice, sending her employees scurrying inside.

"Mrs. Latham, what's the rush?" Beatrice asked as she plunked her large bag down onto the main cutting table.

Her boss scowled. "Let's just say, Mr. Blake is not a patient man and leave it at that."

Tight-lipped as usual. Beatrice sighed. She began to unpack her gear. Pincushion—*check*, scissors—*check*, tape measure—*check*, her coveted set of needles that accompanied her every workday—*check*. Unconsciously, she rubbed her left thumb and forefinger together several times as she looked over at Anna, who was sitting at her desk, elbow planted on its top, watching the entrance.

The door slammed open, and Henry Blake strode into the room, with Mildred mini-stepping and giggling behind him. Beatrice's first thought was, this is not the man Rosie had described a year ago when she first started working with Harris and Blake. Neither retiring nor soft-spoken, the ex-assistant to Harris had a determined countenance and immediately barked orders.

"I want Mildred's dress finished no later than three o'clock this afternoon, got it?" He peered over at Mrs. Latham. "Understand, Mrs. L?" he added.

"Yes, Mr. Blake. I most certainly do," she said icily.

Because Mrs. Latham was usually ultra-polite to her superiors, Beatrice could see this man had obviously gotten under her boss' skin.

With Blake exiting as fast as he had come in, the three seamstresses were abruptly left with a vapid young girl who shifted from one foot to another.

"What do I do first?" she asked, in a breathy, almost childlike voice.

"Stand over here, please," Mrs. Latham directed, "so we can make sure your measurements match what we've already made for you."

The girl giggled nervously. "Don't know what's eating everyone."

Mrs. Latham's eyes bulged. "You don't know what's bothering us, huh?

Perhaps it's because we don't enjoy staying here all day Saturday to work on your dress. A dress, from what Mr. Blake has told me, that won't be needed for at least another week."

The actress gulped. "Sorry."

The girl remained still, rigid, as Mrs. L yanked off her dress, and Anna pulled the almost finished tea green, embroidered, flapper-length gown down over her body. As Beatrice and Anna furiously pinned and snipped, it shifted slightly, making their job more difficult.

But by two o'clock, they were done, Mildred dismissed, and Beatrice and Anna's gear bags packed and ready to go. Mrs. Latham sat at her desk, not so much tired looking as uneasy. Beatrice and Anna exchanged looks.

"Mrs. L, is there something wrong?" Anna asked, breaking the silence.

Their boss nodded. "That man, Blake. I've not said this before, but—"

Beatrice leaned forward. "But?"

Mrs. Latham looked from one to the other. "Did you know that Henry Blake and Chester Harris were lovers?"

Stunned, Beatrice could only manage a soft, "No."

"Oh, yes, and word had it that when the producer's wife discovered the affair, Harris threatened to leave the little so-and-so."

"No!" the seamstresses exclaimed in unison.

"So, he was plenty angry at Harris around the time of the shooting. Besides that, the day before the shooting, I heard from one of the cameramen, that Blake was seen handing a thick enveloped over to a fellow near the main gate in the evening."

"Do the police know about this?" Anna asked.

Mrs. L shrugged. "What difference would that make? They don't seem to care about anything else except filling their own pockets with payoffs from the studios."

"Payoffs?" Beatrice asked softly.

"Yes, bribes. Welcome to good ol' Los Angeles."

Usually, Eddie counted on Mabel's "Pay that idiot no mind." It was her I-don't-give-a-hoot-about-other-people's-opinions that dovetailed so nicely with his own philosophy on the subject. But after being accosted by Henry

Blake, when she handed him the phone, and he heard that all too familiar silence followed by a harsh *click*, nothing she could say would appease him.

"Damn that Blake! I think it's probably been him on the phone. I sensed how much he resented Harris asking me to do his errands. The truth was, everyone knew the two of them had been real cozy together before Harris broke it off. Hopping mad Blake was about it, in fact. He tried to hide it the day before his boss died, but we all knew the scoop."

"I get it that you don't trust that Detective Lozano," Mabel said, "but what about calling his supervisor to tell him? Someone higher up on the ladder, as they say these days."

"Yeah, right. He's got it in for me, too. Who knows? Maybe he's the caller. Fact is, he needs someone—anyone—to arrest so he can make his department look less incompetent than they really are."

She stroked his shoulder. "Honey, you talked to Rosie recently?"

"Yes, early this morning. She told me she was gonna go over to Clara Bow's today, then over to Walt's tonight. She said something about finally seeing his 'Hollywood Room.'"

"What's that, for heaven's sake?"

"He's got himself a collection of Hollywood artifacts, or so he claims."

"Interesting. Maybe I'll go over there myself, and see it sometime."

Eddie chuckled. "Just make sure if you do, to be with Rosie and her mother. Count me out. Her mother isn't my biggest fan." He kissed her on the cheek. "Gotta go now. Lon asked me to help him with a project."

Lon's dogs took one look at Eddie and went crazy. Jumping up on him, barking, wagging their tails furiously, trying to lick any exposed flesh, they were relentless. To make matters worse, when he bent down to pet them, their overactive tongues started to lick his face.

Lon laughed. "You do realize that you've just sabotaged all the lessons in animal good behavior we've been paying for. Where's Rosie, by the way? She gets them even more riled up. She sure has a way with animals, though."

Just then, Hazel entered the hall, dressed in a flowing pair of white "beach" pants, a black chiffon sash, and a dark red puffed-sleeve blouse. "Eddie, so good to see you. No Rosie? I know you two sometimes work on the weekend, but can she possibly make it for dinner, do you think?"

"Nah, she's got plans for tonight, but thanks anyway, Hazel. So nice of you."

Lon put his hand on his protégé's shoulder. "Come on, let me show you what I need."

To a full doggy chorus of yips and barks, the two men retreated down the hall and into Chaney's studio.

Creating a specialized wooden platform to hold all the various masks his mentor owned was both enjoyable and time consuming. Before Eddie knew it, the entire afternoon had flown by, and if Hazel hadn't come in to remind them both to sit down and have a bite of supper, they might have easily gone through the entire evening simply designing, building, and chatting.

"Eat up early. There's always time to work more after supper," she said, wagging her finger.

Both men laughed and followed her into the dining room.

At the dinner table, Hazel turned the conversation from the mundane to more personal things. "Eddie, so when are you and Rosie going to get married?" she asked.

"Hazel!" Lon exclaimed.

Chuckling, Eddie shook his head. "It's all right, Lon. It's a perfectly logical question. Thing is, Hazel, I'd love to marry her tomorrow, but I'm simply waiting for her to make up her mind."

"You two are perfect together. Make up her mind about what, for goodness sake?" Hazel said.

He put down his fork, looked at his hostess and drew a deep breath. "What *she* wants to do with her life, not her mother's idea of it."

February 4, 1926
That Same Saturday, Noon

Unlike the last time Rosie had seen Clara, today the celebrity was in full casual mode—tennis skirt and matching top, soft kidskin shoes with ankle high socks, and a head band nestled into her mass of curly hair.

After a long hug, Rosie said, "I love your outfit, but I didn't know you had a tennis court."

Clara giggled. "Oh, these old rags? Actually, I don't have a court. I just like it as a fashion statement. What do you think?" she asked, twirling around several times before ending up in a mock ballerina's fourth position.

Chuckling, Rosie nodded enthusiastically. "I like it, you crazy lady!"

Their mutual amusement was just what Rosie needed. Such a relief from all the tension brewing over at the Highland Courts ever since she had announced her future plans. Walt hadn't said much, but her mother's anger seeped out everywhere. Drawers banged closed, doors slammed shut, and that morning, when their percolator suddenly stopped working, instead of her usual annoyed comment of, "For goodness sake," Beatrice let out a high-pitched squeal. After that, the constant rubbing of lotion on her fingers up to twenty times a day, told Rosie just how upset her mother still was. Seeing all the old neurotic signs, Rosie didn't dare tell her mother about going over to the infamous actress' house today.

Clara had decided to have a luxurious lunch prepared for her new friend. When two women in full housemaid uniforms carried in trays of mouthwatering food, as well as her valet bringing various cocktails, Rosie clapped her hands with delight. `

"Clara, you're too good to me. What did I ever do to deserve all this marvelous attention?"

Clara smiled. "You are one of the few genuine people I've met ever since I came to Hollywood. Don't think for a minute I don't appreciate it, dear Rosie."

Heartened by that statement, Rosie couldn't stop her pent-up tears. "Clara, I need that more than you know."

The star reached across the table and grasped Rosie's hand. "Tell me what's wrong, honey."

Rosie told her. Everything—the sexual attack, her mother's dogged determination to have her connected with Hollywood at any cost, the pull she has always felt with animals, the explosion that occurred when she announced her true dream. She ended with her frustration at her mother's refusal to accept Eddie.

"Wow. That's a mouthful. No wonder you're crying, sweetie." Clara's eyes had also filled. "As you know, my background was so awful growing up, movies became my godsend. Naturally, that's where I wanted to end up—a huge star. Well, here I am, and it ain't all that grand. Oh, the money is, but when the press and the uppity-ups in Hollywood attack you? Right about now, settling down on a little ranch someplace in Nevada don't seem too bad an idea at all."

Wiping her eyes, Rosie nodded. "Thanks, Clara. That helps a lot."

"Just remember, nobody has the right to take away what your heart wants to do. And that includes being with that handsome Eddie of yours."

When Beatrice arrived home at around four o'clock, she spied the flushed-looking Walt sitting on their front steps. Suddenly, she remembered why he was there. Exhaustion be hanged, finally, here was her chance to see his Hollywood collection. Beaming, she hurried over to him.

"Walt, I'm so looking forward to this!"

He stood up, and swaying back and forth, palmed his hand out toward her. "Sorry, Bea, while you were at work, Rosie called me to say she can't make it this evening. Something came up with a friend of hers who is in trouble, and she has to help her."

"She said what? Which friend and what trouble? You sure she's not just going out with Eddie after all? She knows how much I've wanted to see your collection. I thought she did, too. Sometimes I just don't understand that girl." She paused. "Well, you and I can still see it, right?"

He put his arm around her shoulders, exuding a mix of gin and sweat. "I really wanted to show you both. We can do it another night. But to make it up to you, I got two tickets to see *Flesh and the Devil*, with Greta Garbo. I hope you don't mind, but I contacted your friend Anna, and she said being such a John Gilbert fan, she would love to go see it, too. She'll meet you at Highland's Egyptian movie theater for a five-thirty show."

"Anna? How did you get her telephone number?"

"I didn't. When I went looking for you at Medford, I told her the situation and gave her one of the tickets. Hope you don't mind." He handed her a ticket.

"I suppose it's all right. Frankly, I'd rather see your Hollywood stuff," she said with a pout. "Hey, want to stay for some food beforehand, at least? I've already prepared something for Rosie and me."

He shook his head. "Sorry, dear. I made other plans. We'll do it next week, I promise." With a quick nod, he walked off with an uneven gait.

That Same Saturday Afternoon

His legs up and crossed on top of his desk, Frank leaned back in his chair and glanced at the clock. *Five o'clock.* Then he stared at the bulletin board ten feet away. When he stroked his chin, he felt its stubble, but after last night's bender, shaving had been last thing on his mind when he woke up next to What's Her Name.

Photographs of the Harris case stared back at him. One was of the producer's temple with a large hole in it, another, a close-up of a bullet casing, and a third was of the smudged tracks where probably the killer had walked. Still pinned up, the edges of the pictures were now beginning to curl at their corners and the black images were already well on their way to a coffee brown.

He closed his eyes, his need for sleep overpowering him.

"Frank, there's someone here to see you," his partner said suddenly, interfering with his light doze.

The plump, nondescript middle-aged woman before him seemed visibly upset. *What now.* He pulled himself together enough to swing his legs back onto the floor and stand up.

"What can I do for you, Miss—?"

She put one plump hand on her even plumper hip. "It's Mrs. Bradford, and you've got a lot of nerve."

He blinked. "Pardon?" Another crazy broad like Sheila Morgan, the evangelist follower? He looked over at Shire who shrugged.

"Please, have a seat." He gestured toward the chair adjacent to his desk, and she plopped down hard.

"Now, please tell me why you are so angry, Mrs. Bradford." His head was starting to swim.

"Did anyone tell you I had called weeks ago to give you some very important information?"

Frank blinked again and visualized sleeping in his bed. Trying to be polite was sapping any extra energy he might have. "No. What was the nature of this information?"

"It had to do with the Harris murder case and Eddie Willis."

Jerking into a straight sitting position, Frank asked, "What about him?" He could feel the blood rushing into his head, and out of the corner of one eye, he caught Shire leaning forward.

"I sell coffee and sweets at Medford, Detective Lozano."

"All right. And why would I be interested in this?"

She huffed. "Well, the morning of the—you know—shooting, I was selling coffee and my baked goods, and there was Eddie, buying a coffee from me. For Mr. Harris, he said."

"Look, Mrs. Bradford, I don't quite understand why you are telling me all this. Of course, Eddie worked there so he would probably buy coffee at some point that day."

"Detective, what I'm saying is Eddie was there, buying coffee for Mr. Harris right when the shot rang out."

Frank's heart was pumping so hard and fast, it felt as if it were about to crash out of his chest and catapult into the room.

"So, you see, Eddie Willis is as innocent as you or me!" She stood up. "Just thought you should know. And by the way, you need a better message system."

Rising as well, Frank steadied himself on his desk. "I sure do. My partner here will take your name and information, right, Shire?"

"Yep," Shire said and led Mrs. Bradford over to his side of the desk.

As Frank gathered up his notepad, pencil, and clipboard, Shire stopped his talking with Mrs. Bradford long enough to ask his partner. "Where are you going, Frank?"

"To a now-*proven*-innocent man's house!"

CHAPTER FIFTEEN

"The task I'm trying to achieve, above all, is to make you see."
— D. W. Griffith, director, writer, producer

February 4, 1926
Thirty-one Days AFTER the Harris Shooting
Saturday Evening

FRANK FIGURED HIS hefty banging on Mabel's front door probably wouldn't sit well with her. He was right. When she opened it up a mere four inches, all he could see were two glaring eyes, flaring nostrils, and a distinct snarl on her lips.

"You got some nerve, detective." Her voice sounded like a wad of spit being hurled.

Instantly, he slid one shoe into the opened space. "I need to talk to Eddie. Please, let me in. It's important."

"Detective, enough is enough." She tried to shove the door closed, but when it hit Frank's shoe, it bounced slightly against her hands. He could hear her exhale a soft swear word.

"You don't understand," he said. "I've now got proof that he's off the hook. I just wanted to tell him and…"

"Of course, he's off the hook. What kind of police department you got over there? Eddie ain't here, but I'll be sure to tell him. Now take your damn shoe away."

"Look, Mabel, I need to talk to him. There's a real killer out there somewhere on the lam, and I need to find out anything Eddie can add to shed some light."

At that last line, the door opened up fully, and, if possible, her demeanor looked even more hostile. "Shed some light, you say? Why the hell you guys can't get it right in the first place is beyond me. Always go after the little guy. Never mind that maybe one of the higher ups at the studio hired an assassin. Eddie and others have told me not only was Harris nasty and unpopular, he was also into some sort of racketeering and gambling with the City Hall Gang and the mob. And on top of that, I've heard tell that his ex-lover, Henry Blake, had just been dumped and hopping mad about it. Think about those angles, detective, why don't ya."

Frank nodded. "You're right, I know all about that. We made a mistake. Now, let me speak to Eddie to see if he can remember anything at all, not just about that day. Maybe facts leading up to the shooting that could help me personally find the shooter."

"Help you personally?" She leaned toward him, her strong chicken-soup breath invading his nostrils. "You act like you're working on this case alone."

His sigh exploded. "You could say that, Mabel, you could sure say that. I am on my own, and again, you're right. Many higher ups are probably involved—more than you know." To his relief, he saw her face soften.

"All right, detective. Come on in. He's been at Lon Chaney's all day and probably into the night for dinner. Let me go get Chaney's information from Eddie's address book. You coming?" she asked, already shuffling down the hall toward her boarder's room.

Inside the small chamber, while Mabel combed through Eddie's desk drawers, Frank ratcheted up his police snooping skills. Navigating around the small, neat room, he eyed as many objects as he could—books lying on Eddie's bedside table, an overstuffed chair with a crocheted blanket tossed over it, a small upright bookcase with a few books on carpentry, set building, and mechanics. He also noticed that on the wall, posters of *The Phantom of the Opera* and *The Hunchback of Notre Dame* were prominently displayed.

No surprise there, Frank thought. Both of those flicks had brought Eddie's boss huge success. Frank remembered when he himself had seen those films, and how impressed he had been with the amazing and memorable performances of Chaney with all his creative makeup. In his mind's eye, the man was nothing short of sheer genius.

Wait a minute. Frank suddenly remembered how that family friend, Walt, had spent a few seconds looking at the photographs on top of the bureau. The detective wandered over to them now and stood before the small cluster of pictures. In the background, he could hear Mabel still opening and closing desk drawers as he focused on one of the photographs. It was of Lon Chaney, standing next to Eddie. *Hmm. I wonder…*

"Ah-hah! Here's Chaney's address," she said, pointing to an entry in what appeared to be Eddie's address book.

Frank jotted it down and nodded. "Thanks, Mabel."

She gave him a hard look. "Just be nice to Eddie. I know him. He's the genuine article, the Real McCoy, you know? He sure didn't deserve all that you guys were dishing out."

With the fountain water gurgling in the background, Henry Blake nestled back into his outdoor lawn chaise, a cocktail in his hand, a worried look on his face. The day had not begun well. Nervous to the point of nausea before he left for work, by nightfall, he prayed that the error in judgment he had made just days before Chester Harris was shot, might now be rectified.

Closing his eyes, his mind flitted back to the night he had made that first hastily arranged payoff to one of Miss St. Johns' hired men, out near Medford Studios. *How furious I was back then. How much I wanted to destroy Chester's career, and using Miss St. John's pen power was a surefire way to do it, no matter the cost.*

He opened his eyes now and looked down at his lap, where copies of the two photographs he had originally sent to the famous journalist lay on top of a magazine. The photos were certainly revealing. So, revealing, he originally assumed they would catch the eye of *Photoplay's* "Sob-Sister Confessor of Hollywood," Adela Rogers St. Johns.

One of them was of Harris and himself, arms around each other, up at Julian Eltinge's villa. The second one—courtesy of his manservant, Robert, behind the camera—was of Harris, dressed as a French maid, playing "Movie Time" at Henry's house one hot summer's night.

Apparently, the photos did catch the journalist's eye. But when Henry secretly got word back from her office that she was planning a huge exposé of Harris in her next "The Sob Sister Interview" column, he suddenly got a change of heart. What good would really come out of this article? Chances were Chester Harris would end up unscathed in the end, and he, Henry, the Nobody, would end up out on the street, with empty pockets. Forever.

Thus, came the frantic second meet up with St. Johns' assistant, to stop the article from going forward. Henry shuddered. *That meeting sure cost me a lot of dough, too. After all this, St. Johns better not have written anything.*

Now, with the evening sky melting into its colorful hues, Henry's fingers trembled as he opened up the latest copy of *Photoplay* with Marion Davies on the cover. Slowly, he thumbed through its pages, searching for the kind of article that many in the film industry feared. As he continued on, the anticipation of each new page brought with it, a dry mouth and even dryer lips. And several more sips of his cocktail.

Finally, there it was. St. Johns' column, placed right smack in the middle of the magazine. It was a meaty interview, all right. But it was of the actress Marion Davies, William Randall Hearst's paramour.

Henry leaned back and smiled. *All's well.*

Downtown, another Saturday night celebration of sorts was going on. To be treated by his cousin Tony and Iron Man Ardizzone himself to dinner at the Pacific Dining Car restaurant on West Sixth Street was more than Alonzo felt he deserved. It was a true gesture of high approval, something he had never received before in his life, and although he felt ill at ease, he couldn't help relishing it.

He had never seen such a place. Dark green velvet covered chairs, white tablecloths with elegant silverware and wine goblets on tables next to train windows, each one embellished with rolled up accordion style shades that ended in tassel trimmings. And as an added accent, small wall lamps with matching dark green shades, lent an evening mass-like glow throughout.

Thick slabs of rare steak and potatoes were placed in front of the threesome as all around them, land speculators, real estate tycoons, and fellow bootleggers were having a high old time, celebrating their monetary gains.

No wine there, of course, but into their empty wine glasses gin from pocket flasks were poured. When the wild-haired, slit-eyed Ardizzone raised his glass, Alonzo could feel his pulse jump.

"Here's to you, Alonzo," the mobster said, his wink as broad as his smile.

"Yeah, to you, cousin," added Tony and clinked his glass against Alonzo's.

The three drank the liquor down swiftly, and instantly, Alonzo could feel the room sway slightly. *I have to get better at this*, he thought, as his glass was quickly replenished.

"I gotta say, Alonzo," Ardizzone said, "I had a couple of doubts regarding your taking care of Harris, but you did it. So, here's to a long career ahead of you in our organization. Bravo and salute!"

"Bravo," Tony concurred, with another swig of drink.

By this time, the room was definitely swirling, as the heavy meal, gin, and his sudden angst all combined to bring on full-blown nausea.

"Have go to the restroom," Alonzo muttered and jumping up, knocked his glass over. Racing past the waiters, he could hear in the distance his tablemates howl with laughter. Thankful he made to the toilet, by the time he had thrown up his entire dinner and returned to the table, the bill had been paid, and the two men were standing up, ready to go home. With an uncharacteristic hug goodbye from Ardizzone outside the restaurant, he and Tony were off to Alonzo's cheap Hollywood room.

The ride was spent in total silence, so much so, when Tony pulled over to the curb to let his cousin out, he spoke in a slightly concerned voice. "Still feeling sick? You're so quiet."

Alonzo reached for the car's handle to let himself out, but then he stopped and made a slow swivel around to face his cousin. "The thing is—don't know how to tell you this, but—"

"But what? Spit it out, why don't you? There's no shame in feeling sick, you know. We've all been there."

"No, you don't understand."

"Try me." Tony's voice was tinted with impatience.

"Fact is, I never went to our planned spot that day."

"*What?*"

He gulped. "Yeah, I got to the place you guys had mapped out for me. I had even gone up there once before on my own to practice with my scope. But when the time came for me to do it for real, I chickened out at the last minute. So, when the newspapers came out the next day all about Harris being killed from a rooftop, I just—"

"Yeah, what did you just do?" Tony's face was cloaked in fury.

"I figured at least the job was done by someone, and said nothing."

Although Hazel Chaney was gracious enough to let Frank in straight away, their two dogs were definitely not so accommodating. Growling and yapping, they bounded alongside Hazel and Frank as they went down the hall to Chaney's studio. The dogs' noise grew so loud, Chaney stuck his head out from his workplace.

"What's going on, Hazel?" he asked. Then he caught sight of Frank. "What the hell do you want now?"

"I need to see Eddie Willis. Is he here?"

"Not for the likes of you, he isn't," Lon snarled.

Eddie's voice from inside the room carried out into the hall. "What, him again?"

"Please, I know Eddie's innocent. Just let me talk to him, all right?" Frank asked.

Lon, rooted in a broad pose, tightened his arms across his chest. Eddie came up behind him and said quietly, "Let him in."

Chaney relaxed his stance and stood aside to let the detective enter.

Inside the studio, Frank immediately apologized. "Look, I know we were rough on you, Eddie, but you gotta understand the pressure we were under. After all—" The detective stopped and stared at a framed photograph on the wall next to him, showing a small group of people. "What is this?" he asked slowly.

Walking over to it, he placed his index finger on one of the figures standing next to Lon Chaney. "You know Walt?"

Chaney nodded. "Yeah? So?"

"Lon, you never told me you knew Walt," Eddie added.

"How do you know him, and why is he standing next to you?" Frank asked, his eyes and voice on alert.

"Let's sit down, shall we?" Lon motioned them both over to a chair and small sofa enclave, located off to one side of his studio.

"Eddie, it never occurred to me to mention Walt because I didn't think it would mean anything to you. Why does it?" Chaney asked.

"He's Rosie's superintendent, and someone they treat like family." Frank noticed Eddie's voice sounded somewhat cautious.

Lon looked startled. "They do? Oh, that's not a good thing. Not at all."

Bypassing Eddie's stunned face, Frank took over. "Tell us why, Mr. Chaney. Again, how did you know him?"

Chaney leaned back amongst the sofa pillows and blew a puff of air out of his mouth. "About ten years ago, Walt Madison worked with me for about two years. He became my right-hand man back then, doing carpentry, helping me out with my makeup. Anything I needed, really. He wasn't the caliber that you are, Eddie, by any stretch of the imagination, but he was important enough to make me concerned when tragedy hit him so hard."

He paused to let that sink in. "When his wife and daughter were killed in a trolley car accident two days before his son went off to fight in the Great War, he simply fell apart. He couldn't sleep, he couldn't eat, and his endless tears and sobs made me fear for his sanity." He paused again. "Meanwhile, the studios decided to place him in the Slatterton State Hospital. Chamber of horrors was more like it. It was terrible. I visited him numerous times, and each time it seemed the hospital staff had put him through some new treatment or experiment. Things like giving him multiple icy cold baths a day and restraining him to the tub. I was there once when he tried to climb out of the bath. I actually heard the attendant snarl at him, 'Shut up if you know what's good for you!' then shove him back into the chilled water.

"Another thing they tried was Somnifen, a drug they used to make him sleep. And sleep he did. He slept so much, they had a hard time waking him up for meals. When I brought that to their attention, their blank faces and slight smirks were frightening. They simply replied, 'Speak to the director. He's the ruler around here.'"

"Good God," Frank murmured.

Lon nodded. "But to top things off, the director decided to put him on a Malaria routine—injecting him with the virus, then treating him for it. Well, he was never the same after that."

"How so?" Eddie asked.

"After he was released, I hired him back, of course. But his concentration wasn't nearly what it had once been. Except for anything he had a gripe about. Then he'd get completely fixated on whatever got his attention and not let it go."

Frank leaned over, his elbows on his knees. "What kind of gripes are we talking about here?"

"Well, for one thing, he kept going down to the local military office and making a damn nuisance of himself, yelling about our boys dying over in France and asking how was the army going to protect them better. At one point, I had to actually go down there and drag him home, and that's when I saw empty bottles of gin all over his apartment—everywhere I looked.

"And then when he got word his son had died in France, well, he became so much worse. He was so proud of his son, you know. I had met him before he enlisted—nice boy. All Walt's worry and his son dies. Ironic, really."

"Why's that?" Frank asked, wondering where all of this was leading.

"For all Walt's demands of the army, the fact is his son probably would have been safer than a lot of the boys in the trenches."

"Why would he be safer?" Eddie asked.

"Because he was a sharp shooter. It seems they got special treatment. And according to Walt, he was a real good shot, too."

Frank cleared his throat. "Excuse me, Mr. Chaney, this is all interesting, but—"

Just then, Hazel entered with a tray of coffee and cookies. Eddie and Chaney smiled at her, but Frank went deeper into his thoughts.

Walt's son was a sharp shooter. Interesting, but not necessarily a link to anything. Looks like Walt was just a poor slob with a hard luck story.

"Detective Lozano, you started by saying I was off the hook. So why are you really here?" Eddie demanded.

"First off, I wanted to tell you that the woman at the Medford coffee stand came to the station and told me how you were there buying coffee for Harris at the time of the shooting."

"Yeah, well, I told you about that right off, didn't I?"

Frank nodded. "Yeah, you did."

"And by the way, I never did get my special jacket back from the crime scene," Eddie added angrily.

"What?" Frank asked.

"My uncle's World War I bombardier jacket, which meant a lot to me. My father had given it to me after my uncle died. It had a British medal that my uncle had removed from a fallen soldier pinned on the collar. When they took Harris to the morgue, it went with him. I never saw it again."

"You mean that flight jacket didn't belong to Harris?"

Eddie's laugh was tinged with cynicism. "You kidding? He'd never wear something like that. No, he was chilled that day, and when he told me to go get him coffee, he insisted I give it to him for warmth while I got him coffee. Wore it with the collar up, he was so cold. Then I was supposed to go back to his office and pick up his suit jacket and bring it back to him lickety-split."

Frank went pale. "Oh, my God."

"What, detective?" Lon asked.

"The evangelist, Aimee Simple McPherson, actually said it."

"What?" chorused Eddie and Lon.

"Something I put down to psychic hocus-pocus. She said that the bullet in the Harris shooting was meant for someone else, not the producer. In other words, the shooter got the wrong man."

It was Eddie's turn to become pale. "What are you saying, detective?"

"I think that bullet was meant for you, Eddie."

"Who would want to kill me?"

Lon started muttering, "Dear, oh, dear." He slowly looked over at Eddie. "You told me Walt was very close to Rosie and her mother, right?"

Eddie nodded.

"Well, when Walt's son died, he received a few belongings from him, and the boy's sharpshooter rifle was one of them."

"He had a long-range rifle?" Frank asked.

"Yeah. There's something else. I didn't say this before, but the main reason I had to get rid of Walt was for a very different reason than I told you before."

"We're listening," Frank said.

"He became obsessed with Aida, one of my female makeup artists. Wouldn't leave her alone. Oh, he didn't want to date her, Aida claimed. At first, he was just being kind to her. Really kind. Helped her with my assignments and always supported her, with great understanding and calm. But then he changed. He began stalking her after work. He was also really nasty to any guy who came near her. He'd call them up on the phone at night, then hang up—that kind of thing."

"How did you know that?" Frank asked.

Lon sighed. "He bragged about it once," he said. "Anyway, my helper claimed he told her because Julia, his own daughter, had died, that Aida was his 'true' daughter, all grown up. Threatened to kill her if she ever left him. Well, as you can imagine, with no help from the police, Aida couldn't take it any longer and decided to leave Los Angeles in the dead of night."

"How strange," Eddie said. "Telephoned them at night, huh? I wonder—nah, it couldn't be. Why, he's considered like family to Rosie and her mother."

Lon grimaced. "Family, you say? Well, that's what he told Aida all the time. He even had a rhyming nickname for her, which I heard him use a lot."

"Yeah? What was that?" Frank asked.

"Aida-Paida."

Eddie leapt up and started for the door.

"What the hell, Willis?" Frank shouted after him.

Eddie stopped and flipped around. "Walt always calls Rosie, Rosie-Posey. And Rosie told me that she had just recently told her mother and Walt how she's quitting Hollywood forever. Possibly even leaving town."

"Then Rosie—" Frank started.

"Could be in danger, yes!"

Rushing out of the room together, Frank barked, "Get in my car, Willis! We'll go together!"

Rosie was glowing. An afternoon of such warmth and support from Clara, a bolstering of her inner desires and now a luxurious ride home by Clara's personal chauffeur, Felix, was just the ticket. If nothing else, she felt certain things would work out. At the curb, she thanked the amicable chauffeur, who insisted on opening her car door for her. She shook his hand and walked toward her apartment.

Humming slightly, she was taken by surprise when Walt suddenly stepped out from behind Highland's archway.

"Walt! I almost forgot about our plans. Let me just wash my face off, and then you, Mama, and I can go see your special exhibit."

Walt cleared his throat. "Ah, Rosie, dear, your mama got called in at the last minute to do a costume tailoring. She wanted me to tell you she's so sorry."

Rosie sighed. "Poor Mama. They work her to the bone, don't they?"

He nodded slowly.

"I guess we'll go another time, like next week, maybe?" she said.

"If you're here next week," he muttered.

She rested her hand on his arm. "Now, Walt. Nothing's happening that fast."

"Anyway, I thought I'd take you there now," Walt said. "I'll do another special tour for your mother next week."

"I thought you wanted to take us both together."

"A man can change his mind, can't he?" He smiled crookedly. "I'd like to give each of my special ladies a separate command performance." He offered her his arm. "So, shall we?"

He smelled of gin, and suddenly, she wasn't sure she wanted to go without Beatrice being present. "Walt, I'm kind of tired. Why don't we wait for Mama?" She stepped back a pace.

An overwhelming urge to go inside and cuddle with Patches and Ginger in bed while she read came over her. But looking at his crestfallen face, she felt a stab of guilt. *After all he's done for us, I can't disappoint him now.*

Gently, she wrapped her hand around his arm. "Okay. I need to do one quick thing inside, and then you can lead on, Mr. Hollywood Prop Master."

"Okay, hurry up. Rosie-Posey, I guarantee you, this will be something you'll never forget."

CHAPTER SIXTEEN

*"Anyone who has a continuous smile on his face
conceals a toughness that is almost frightening."*
— Greta Garbo, actress

**February 4, 1926
Thirty-one Days AFTER the Harris Shooting
The Night Continues**

FUMBLING WITH HIS key, Walt dropped it twice then had trouble inserting it into the lock. Rosie slowly shook her head. *When did he become so old, so bumbling?* Standing behind him, she also got a hefty whiff of his gin cologne, so evident these days. The sudden sadness of that fact, hit her hard.

"It's about time you let me see your Hollywood collection," she said, her voice far more chipper than she felt. "Won't Mama be hopping mad I got to see it first."

He produced a slight smile. "Yes, I suppose so."

Inside the door, it was pitch black, and immediately, he placed a hand on her arm. "Wait, stay here until I can turn on some lights."

The general waft of alcohol invaded her senses, as if instead of a good douse of soap and water, the room had been cleansed with it. *This is not good. Better tell Mama. Well, she'll see this for herself next Saturday.*

He seemed to stumble forever, knocking into furniture, cursing when he obviously had kicked over an empty bottle on the floor. She heard a *roll–clink, roll–clink* off somewhere and wondered how many other bottled-companions might also be resting on the floor.

Finally, a light was turned on, then another, and the room was exposed.

It was a living room, but off hand, she didn't notice many props, or costumes. Although it certainly didn't look sparse per se, she had expected more Hollywood-oriented things in it.

"This is nice, Walt," she lied. "Don't know why you haven't invited us over before this."

Shrugging, he drew a deep breath. "Always liked your place better, I guess." He indicated the sofa and she sat down.

"So, is this the special Hollywood room?" she asked.

He stared at her a beat before answering. "No, we'll get to that, I promise. Gotta go to the bathroom first. Stay put, all right?"

He left the room. She could hear him colliding into the wall a couple of times, probably going down a hallway. Once he was out of sight, she got up to explore. It turned out there were quite a few Hollywood mementos, after all. Numerous headshots of actors and actresses, some signed, some not, covered one of his walls, and it was interesting checking them out. Ethel Barrymore, Harold Lloyd, Tallulah Bankhead, Joe E. Brown, and Buster Keaton all stared forward in posed positions. A wooden camera tripod stood off in one corner, and a couple of tall, wide-brimmed hats were nailed to the wall. *From a Tom Mix cowboy movie?* She reached up and fingered one of the brims, then smelled her fingers. Now they, too, smelled of liquor.

Continuing with her tour of the room, she noticed various books on the Wild West, dozens of murder mysteries, and several old dime novels from the 1800s. *These might really be worth something.* She continued looking. Over on a side table was Walt's faithful companion, the Brownie camera, the one he had bought in 1919, the one that never seemed to leave his hands.

Pictures, she suddenly thought. Did he have any personal photographs around? She turned to probe some more. She saw quite a few across the way on top of a wall shelf, and was about to scope them out, when she was suddenly taken by a large, opened mahogany box of letters with a photograph of a young woman attached to its inside top. Upon closer look, the girl was attractive, and she was holding up a mask similar to what Rosie had seen in Lon Chaney's studio. Her eyes then shifted down into the box itself. Filled with letters addressed to someone named Aida, she opened up one of the envelopes. The letter started out, To My Darling Daughter. Was this the daughter who was killed? Wasn't she a child when that happened, and wasn't her name Julia?

She shrugged and put the envelope back. A short stride over to the wall shelf soon had her studying several photographs. There was a nice picture of Walt and Beatrice in front of the courtyard, his arm around her mother's shoulders, both smiling broadly. She chuckled, remembering how Walt had asked her to take that photograph. How happy they all were back then. Next was a photograph of him and Lon Chaney. *What? He knows Lon? How come he never mentioned that?* There was a picture of herself in the courtyard obviously going to work. Next up, another photo of herself armed with her satchel, on her way to the market; another one of her in the evening, under the glow of the Highland Court's outside lamp. Then was another, and another, and another. At least ten more—all of them, of her.

She could feel gooseflesh forming. Why so many of just her? And worse, taken without her knowledge. Picking up one more, she noticed Walt had written across it, like a famous star's autograph, "To my Rosie-Posey."

When she heard his footsteps back in the room, she jumped.

"I see you've been looking around," he said behind her. But it wasn't in his normal Walt voice. It was colder, with a slight edge to it.

When she turned to face him, she winced. *Did he drink even more in the bathroom?* His face was red and sweaty, and his panting brought with it more blasts of gin. She felt like gagging, yet somehow, from deep inside her, she grabbed at some normalcy.

"Walt, this is all fine, but I thought you would have more items. But thanks for showing me. I should go."

He came close, his shirt showing blotches of perspiration, particularly under his armpits.

"This isn't the main attraction, my dear. Not by any means. It's over there, through that closed door."

"Walt, I don't know about this." Her heartbeats were fluttering fast now, as fast as the hummingbird wings she had once watched.

He curled his large hand around her forearm and pressed down. "Come on, stick around. I was just about to show you the main attraction."

She opened her mouth to protest, but only jerky breaths slipped out. When he drew her across the room with him, she felt powerless, like the rag doll she had as a child. They stopped in front of a door with a solid brass

Master pad lock. Off to the right of the door was a lone key on an embedded wall hook. To the left of it was a rifle leaning against the wall in a nearby corner, next to a small basket of what appeared to be dusty towels and rags.

She looked at the rifle standing up in the corner. "Whose is that?" she blurted out.

"It was my son's. A present from the good ol' United States army. God bless America," he muttered bitterly.

To ward off her growing fear, she searched for a way to temper his mood. "Sorry, Walt. I know how much you loved your boy."

That seemed to distract him, and watching his shoulders relax, she tried to think rationally. *This is Walt, for goodness sake. He would never hurt you.*

The lock opened fast, as if well oiled, and they were both inside another blackened room, this one chillier than the living room and surprisingly odor free.

"Wait a second—here it is," Walt said, and with an odd clicking sound, the room was suddenly lit up. A single bulb screwed into the low ceiling with a dangling pull string flashed its yellow light, blinding Rosie for a second or two. Then her eyes acclimated. She blinked twice and let her eyes sweep around the room.

"Oh—my—God," she murmured and cupped her mouth.

Frank and Eddie's syncopated pounding on the Paige's door echoed throughout the quiet neighborhood. Standing side by side, they were relentless until Beatrice flung open the door to snarl at them.

"What in the world is going on?" she snapped. "I'm in no mood to deal with you two."

"Where's Rosie?" Eddie asked.

"Isn't she with you, Eddie?" Beatrice asked. "Walt told me she was helping a friend, but I figured that was just a lie she had told him."

"Walt! Where is he?" Frank demanded.

"Don't know, and frankly, I'm annoyed at him right now. He sent me on a wild goose chase tonight. Told me a colleague of mine would be at the movies, waiting for me. But she was a no-show."

Suddenly Frank looked beyond her and pointed to something. "What's that on your wall mirror?"

Beatrice turned. "Why, it's a note from Rosie. That's where we leave our messages for each other because—"

Already charging over to the mirror, Eddie pulled the paper out of the frame's edge. A fast read, and he handed it over to the detective.

"Rosie's with Walt. Where does he live?" Frank barked.

"Why are you both so upset?" She clutched at Eddie's arm. "Tell me what's happening!"

Eddie looked down at her. "We think Rosie's in danger, Mrs. Paige. Please, give us Walt's address."

"Rosie in danger? From Walt? I don't understand." She started to cry.

Frank exploded. "His address. Now!"

Quivering, she nodded and gave him the exact address. "It's not far. Eight blocks down, five blocks west. Oh, Rosie," she wailed as Eddie hopped into Frank's car and readied it for the detective. Frank gave it a good crank, then, leaping back into the driver's seat, he revved it up into a growl, and they were off, the burn of tire rubber blasting behind them into the night.

In Walt's room, a kind of shrine had been set up, with a large photograph of her in a gold frame at its epicenter. On either side of her picture were unlit candles in iron wall holders. On the wall, off to the right of her portrait, and completely covered in a bed sheet, sat a large, three-dimensional object with odd little shapes protruding out from the middle of it.

The lump in the back of her throat was making it difficult to swallow.

"This is the Grand Finale," he said. He turned toward one of the walls and pointed. "Let's start over here." Although his voice was somewhat back to normal, it sounded commanding.

He steered her over to a wall that had various small pieces of paper taped to it, all of them organized in different fanned out groupings. Within each group, there was a similar logo at the top of each sheet: The Buccaneer Group, with a two-digit address in the San Fernando Valley area.

"What are these?" she said, her voice wobbling slightly.

"Look more closely, and I'll tell you." He pushed her closer to the little papers.

She noticed he had signed each one and most of the dates were on the weekends, either a Saturday or Sunday.

"You know what that means?" he asked, his eyes blazing slightly. "It means I was there on those dates." To Rosie, he looked almost smug.

"I thought you were with your friend in the hospital on weekends."

His lips curled up at the edges, but his eyes were dull, emotionless. "That's what I told you, all right."

She thought of her mother, so trusting of Walt. *Why would he lie to her?*

Still holding her with a firm grip, he took her over to another part of the wall. There, two photos had been placed far apart and each one sat next to a small, faded newspaper byline.

"Recognize these two fellas?"

She leaned in close to study the first photograph. "It's—" She choked. Both of her knees gave way under her.

Walt caught her and propped her up. "That's right, it's Mark Oliver. Alongside of you."

"I don't understand." Tears were forming.

"You know I always take pictures. To prove how wrong you are."

"Me, wrong? Walt, I don't understand," she repeated. After she leaned close to read the short paragraph that was placed next to Mark's photograph, she started to cry in earnest. "He was killed?"

Walt snorted. "He was no good for you, Julia."

"Julia? Walt, it's me, Rosie. Please stop," she pleaded.

"Next up: Willy Sweet. Now *he* was a handsome lad." Tiny beads of perspiration danced across his brow.

It was a photo of Willy and her going out on one of their dates. Next to their picture was another small byline about how he was shot to death with a rifle. "Killer still at large," it read. Her tears kept coming as she flashed on all the good times they had together.

He let go of her hand, and she instinctively stepped back, her voice coming out in tiny gasps.

"Walt. I—" She started to back away from him. "Did you kill both of them? *Why?*"

Dripping sweat now, his eyes bore into her with such intensity, she had trouble breathing.

"My son should have returned home. Mark did. Willy did."

"You killed them because they were alive, and your son was dead?"

He looked at her as if stunned at her reasoning. "No, of course not."

"Then, why?"

"Don't you see? They had to be killed. They both were gonna take you away from me. You were taken away from me once, Julia. I couldn't let that happen again."

She held onto a chair to stop from falling. "Walt, I'm not Julia, I'm Rosie!"

He didn't bat an eye. "Here's the presentation I promised you," he went on, "With the worst of them all." Stepping over to the cloth-covered item, he whipped the sheet off and flung it to the floor.

She let out a strangled moan.

Going at a forty-five miles-per-hour breakneck speed, Frank and Eddie were making good time. Until they weren't.

An old man, clutching his cane, and paying no attention to the world around him, decided to step down from the curb at the exact moment the Ford was barreling around the corner.

"Christ! What was that?" Frank yelled after the impact.

He swerved the car over to the curb and stopped. With the motor still puttering, both of them jumped out and ran back a few yards to see. The man, sprawled out on the ground, was better than expected, but with no time to waste, Eddie got aggressive.

"I'm going on by foot," he said and turned to go.

"Wait, stop! Here's someone coming now. I'll flag him down," Frank said breathlessly as a car approached.

The automobile braked. As soon as the detective ran over and explained the situation, the driver stepped out of the driver seat and together with Frank, hoisted the moaning victim into his car. The good Samaritan rumbled down the street, and the detective hopped back into his car, with Eddie croaking, "Let's go, let's go!" every few seconds.

Rosie stared at a giant dartboard on the wall. Pinned to its center was Eddie's photograph, his phone number scrawled across his neck in thick, black digits. Worse still, was the tight cluster of darts sticking out of his face––his eyes, his nose, his mouth, even a random dart hurled at his Adam's apple.

"Eddie," Walt snarled. "I thought I had him. But I didn't and all because Harris was wearing Eddie's damn bombardier jacket with the collar up. Couldn't get a clear look at his face. Well, I'll get him next time. No more calling him at night to rattle him, either. I'm just gonna shoot him down like a dog."

She looked at Walt's face. It was unrecognizable. The person they called family was completely gone. With his eyes bulging almost out of their sockets, his hair matted down with sweat, he had become a madman.

She broke free of him and ran toward the door.

"Oh no, you don't. I'm sick to death of people leaving me!" He came after her. Grabbing her by the arm, he yanked her to him. Then, twisting his torso around, he went for something behind his back.

It was a handgun.

That's when she screamed, "Help!" with all her might.

Outside the house, Eddie and Frank heard her and sprang into action. Without talking, they each instinctively did whatever they had to do to get inside. Eddie charged toward the back, Frank, his gun out and cocked, bounded toward the side of the house.

"Help!" Rosie cried again, as Eddie frantically tried hurling his muscular body against the back door. He didn't even make a dent.

"Willis, come here!" Frank called out. Barreling over, Eddie could see Frank, his jacket wrapped around his hand and arm, bashing in a low-lying window. "I can tell she's near here," the detective hissed.

Crunching over broken glass, Eddie elbowed off some of the remaining shards still attached to the window frame. Then, one by one, they climbed through. Inside was some sort of storeroom, with dusty boxes, furniture, and a standing lamp.

Another "Help!" came through the walls, clear as a bell.

Frank motioned a this-a-way signal with his head, gripping his gun with two hands now, as he approached a door on the east side of the room. Leaning against it, he listened. When Rosie moaned a weak "Help," he and Eddie both nodded.

"Together on three, all right?" Frank whispered to Eddie.

"One-two-three!" Frank barked and swinging backward, they both booted hard against the door.

It worked. Barging into the room, they slammed on their brakes to a full halt.

Across from them, in front of the other door, Rosie was there with Walt behind her, his gun to her head.

Instantly, Eddie saw Frank embrace a negotiating mode. "Look, Mr. Madison, Walt, we're not here to arrest you. Just put the gun down before anyone gets hurt."

Walt snickered. "You really think I'm worried about getting arrested? You're stupider than I thought."

"What do you want, Walt?" Eddie asked, taking in every ounce of panic on Rosie's face.

Walt glowered. "For one thing, I wanted you dead, Eddie. For another, Rosie is coming with me. She's my daughter, and I have a right to keep her."

He's gone plumb crazy. Eddie watched Walt wave his Colt around twice.

"Walt, I want to go home," Rosie mewed.

"You are home, Julia. Don't you know that by now?" Walt said, and pressed the gun's barrel harder against her ear.

Julia? He's completely gone.

Eddie could hear the hammer click of Frank's gun. *Here we go. I'll grab Rosie once Walt's down.* He waited for the crack of the detective's gun.

It came—from the wrong source. *Damn!* Frank was down on the floor, grabbing his shoulder, his police issue weapon flung away from him.

"Still think you can stop me?" Walt growled, his grip even tighter around Rosie. "You're next Willis. Finally, I can get the job done!"

Again, Eddie noticed when Walt talked, his gun left her head as he waved it around to emphasize his point.

Out of the corner of his eye, he could see Frank struggling to scrape his way over to his gun, a couple of yards away.

Walt snarled, "Willis, you think you're gonna take her home with you, huh?"

"I guess you're right," Eddie said, placating him. "After all, she is your daughter, your Rosie-Posey."

Walt waved his gun upward. "You're damn right, she's my—"

Lunging at him, Eddie grabbed Walt by the collar and gave him a hefty punch to the face, allowing just enough time to shove Rosie out of harm's way. Stunned, Walt recovered quickly, and the two men began a struggle to control the gun. Twisting, grappling, they both held onto the Colt, like two wrestlers, both using every ounce of strength they had, neither of them letting go.

Walt, a frenzied powerhouse by now, was beginning to gain the upper edge, and for all his strength as a young man, Eddie could feel his own grip weakening. *Am I gonna die here? No! Gotta save Rosie* kept him going, but Walt was bending his hand back so far, the pain stabbed him like a serrated knife.

Off to the side, Rosie screamed, "Get him, Eddie, get him!" but he knew he was losing ground.

Suddenly, with a huge grunt, Walt managed to shift the gun around to an inch from Eddie's chest. *This is it. I'm gonna die.*

"Duck, Eddie!" Frank yelled.

Eddie ducked, and the crack of the detective's gun ripped through the room.

Instantly, Walt fell backward, taking Eddie with him.

It took Eddie a couple of seconds to realize what had happened. Crushed against Walt's sweat-soaked shirt, he pushed himself up, just in time to see the life go out of the man's eyes.

"Oh, Eddie," Rosie sobbed, and in a flash, he was standing up with her in his arms.

"Rosie, Rosie," he said between kisses, "I thought I'd lost you."

Crying, she kissed him back. "I love you, I love you," floated through the air.

Off to one side, Frank wiped his eyes with the back of his sleeve, then cleared his throat.

They both came over to him.

"Thank you, detective. You save our lives," Eddie said, grasping Frank's hand hard.

Rosie simply threw her arms around the detective. "Yes, thank you, thank you," she whispered in his ear.

Frank nodded and drew the longest sigh Eddie had ever heard. "Look, Eddie," he said, "you played a big hand in this, you know. Couldn't have done it without you." He looked down at Walt. "Let's wrap this up, shall we?"

All three started to walk out into Walt's living room, when Eddie stopped.

He had caught sight of his face and phone number.

"My God. All this time it was Walt," he said.

Frank cocked his head. "Yes, Eddie, I think we established that."

"Phone calls at night, detective, that's what I'm talking about. Thought it was probably you."

"The only person I call at night is my partner," Frank said. "And then I'm usually drunk."

Out in Walt's living room, Frank picked up the phone. Dialing it in, he winked at the two of them with their arms wrapped around each other, Rosie's head rested against Eddie's chest.

"Captain Billings? I caught the Harris killer…yeah…yeah I will…no, this is someone you don't know…here's the address…"

After he hung up, he turned to the couple. "As soon as they come, I'll take you two home. In the meantime, why don't you both wait for me in my car?"

Later, after the police had arrived, the body taken away on a stretcher, the neighbors gawking nonstop, their horror replaced by exhaustion, Eddie and Rosie were more than ready to have Frank take them home. But he drove only ten seconds before he suddenly stopped in the middle of the street. Rotating around toward the two of them cuddled together in the cramped back seat, he smiled, a mischievous look on his face.

"Hey, you two lovebirds. It just occurred to me—"

They both looked at him.

"Here's one for the movies. Hurray for Hollywood."

EPILOGUE

*"I love her and that's the beginning and
the end of everything."*
— F. Scott Fitzgerald, author

March 4, 1926
Fifty-nine Days AFTER the Harris Shooting
Saturday, 3 p.m.

BEFORE THE WEDDING even started, Minister Joshua Bennett couldn't stop grinning. Brought in from faraway Fillmore for the occasion, he looked around at the small assemblage gathered in Mabel's crowded living room and smiled. *No one is going to believe me when I tell them who is here today!*

Having talked to the groom a mere three weeks earlier, Eddie had informed him that since downtown City Hall these days, what with all its corruption, was the last place he wanted to have his wedding, it would please him no end to have his hometown minister drive to Los Angeles with his parents to officiate their vows and publicly give them his blessing.

As the room hummed with conversation, punctuated by snorts of laughter, Bennett understood the groom was due to enter any moment now. And as for the bride? Rumor had it she was holed up with her mother in an undisclosed location.

That location turned out to be Mabel's bedroom, but for Rosie and Beatrice, it might as well have been Omaha, many years before. After the loop-the-loop rollercoaster implosion of Walt, Beatrice had trouble coping. Too many reminders of past deceptions and loss, she told Rosie, each time her daughter inquired how she was doing.

No words had been spoken when Rosie informed her of Eddie's and her wedding. Each time Rosie mentioned it, a brusque nod was all Beatrice would give. Nor did Beatrice speak much when she worked tirelessly through several nights to finish Rosie's stylish wedding dress.

Still, in spite of everything, her mama hadn't lost her touch. Studying herself in the mirror today, Rosie welled up. "Your work is so beautiful, Mama," she said softly.

A lace head cap with tiny satin flowers kept her red curls in check, as the attached veil flowed down over her flapper-style gown. This time, Rosie didn't have to worry about her mama getting in trouble. Mrs. Latham had gifted all the fabrics. And to top things off, around her neck were her mother's borrowed pearls, along with her newly acquired matching earrings from Clara, which sparkled and glowed in the light each time she moved.

She had to say something, no matter how her mama was feeling. This was supposed to be the most important day of her life and not to have any words between them left her feeling crushed, far beyond the shock and loss of Walt.

Beatrice glanced over at Mabel's bureau top, where the landlady's mahogany Westchester clock was clicking toward three o'clock. "I suppose we should get going," she said simply and made a move toward the door.

Rosie couldn't take it any longer. She grabbed her mother's arm. "Mama, please. We need to discuss something now."

"Discuss what?"

"How you hate Eddie, and you don't want me to marry him."

To Rosie's surprise, her mother paused, an almost thoughtful look across her face. She shook her head. "You know, Rosie, truth be told, obviously I'm not such a good judge of character. Probably never was. But today I woke up thinking about something that was completely unexpected."

Rosie released her mother's arm. "What was that, Mama?"

"I was thinking that people aren't what they seem. Well, we sure saw that with Walt, didn't we? I also thought about your father, the studio heads, the stars and the nothing bit players, and I realized that when push comes to shove, you're actually not so bad off. Maybe Eddie is not exactly like your father, after all."

"Oh, Mama!" Rosie cried, flinging her arms around the seamstress. They held onto each other like that several minutes, until the clock chimed three times. Their eyes splashed with tears, they stepped back from each other and simultaneously, gently dabbed at their eyes so as not to smear any makeup. Then with linked arms, they went off to the main attraction.

"Here she is," Mabel called out and immediately, one of her renters started playing Mendelssohn's *Wedding March* on his Hohner One Row button accordion.

After coming down the "aisle" with her mother, Rosie stood next to her future husband and smiled, as Beatrice took a seat. He looked so handsome, so in love, she wondered why she had ever doubted him at all. Reverend Bennett opened his Bible and the crowd hushed, but she couldn't help herself. She had to tell Eddie something. She leaned in even closer to him.

"Eddie," she whispered, "I had my dream last night."

The minister cleared his throat loudly.

"Did it turn out okay?" Eddie whispered back.

Several murmurs floated through the room.

"It sure did. That unknown man? Not the bad ones, the kind one? It was *you!*"

Smiling, Eddie winked.

"Are we ready?" Bennett asked kindly, an amused smirk on his face.

When they both nodded, he began.

Beatrice started to cry, but as soon as Frank handed her his handkerchief with a pat on her hand, she smiled.

As per their instructions, the ceremony was brief and to the point. No flowery words, only mutual statements of love from each of them, along with the usual, *Do you take this man? Do you take this woman?* No Bible passages, no asking if anyone objected, because at the time the reverend was hired, Rosie was worried Beatrice's grimacing face might ruin the day.

After Eddie kissed Rosie to the sound of several sighs and one or two claps, they turned to their guests and graciously accepted all the cheers and applause.

But it was Mabel who said it best. "Listen up, folks, listen up. Let's all have something to eat, and a lot of champagne!"

Frank immediately burst out with, "I'll drink to that!" bringing on a roar of approval.

From out of nowhere, champagne bottles were brought forth faster than the best speakeasies in town. Next came platter after platter of finger sandwiches, which, as Mabel proudly announced, were like "having tea with British royalty!"

Rosie's fellow bit players were flirting outrageously with Frank and his partner, Shire; Beatrice was embroiled in a long conversation with Eddie's parents; Lon and Clara were head-to-head, laughing; the veterinarian, Dr. Peterson and Hazel were busy stroking Patches and Ginger, and the newlyweds were suddenly sitting in the corner all alone.

"Happy, sweetheart?" Eddie asked between sandwiches.

Rosie smiled. "You have no idea." She was about to relate her conversation with her mama and the hope that things might one day work out between them, but she never got the chance.

Mabel, once again, was in charge and obviously having a whale of a time doing it. Her face was flushed, her hair, tousled from nonstop movement, and her filled-to-the-brim flute was held up high. In her other hand, was a medium-sized megaphone.

"Before we have cake, it's time for some speeches," she blasted away. People spilled their drinks and dropped their food at the sudden sound impact, followed by a wave of laughter.

First Mabel looked over at Beatrice, then Eddie's parents. "Are any of you up for starters?" she asked. His parents appeared slightly nervous. Beatrice, her eyes flashing, didn't look happy.

Oh dear, Mama's regretting this. I guess she's not fully on board. Rosie tried to let go of the sinking feeling in her gut.

Eddie's father coughed once and nodded. He held his glass up high as well. "Congratulations to the bride and groom! And Rosie, we look forward to getting to know you better when you both come to live in Fillmore."

More applause. Mabel's eyes swept the small crowd. "Next?"

Clara stepped up, her simple sheath becoming, her famous flashing dark eyes, coquettish, and her expression, completely infectious.

"Rosie, Eddie, all I can say is, I think you're the luckiest people alive. You have a fine head start in this crazy, cockeyed world, and with your great love and support for each other, I just know you'll succeed. So, here's to you both. Bottoms up, everyone!" The room tingled with the repeated sound of glasses clinking.

"Who's next?" Mabel asked and zeroed in on Frank.

"You giving me the Evil Eye?" he asked her, to several guffaws. "All right, then. Here's one for the ages. Eddie? Rosie? All I can say is, you both give me hope."

"Aw," rippled through the crowd.

Lon was next. "I have something to add, if I might."

The room hushed.

"From the moment I met Eddie, I knew he was someone special. As much as I'll miss him around here, I'm glad he's going to return to his family and his roots."

Worried, Rosie glanced over at Beatrice. They hadn't actually discussed her moving away. Every time she tried to talk about it, Beatrice would change the subject.

"But I also knew Rosie was terrific the moment Hazel and I met her. We knew she was the perfect gal for Eddie, and in light of the fact that she not only adores animals—frankly, we think she's a magician with them—I've taken it upon myself to help this couple out."

"What have you done, Lon?" Eddie asked, speaking low.

The makeup artist pulled an envelope out of his pocket and handed it over to the newlyweds. "This is just Hazel's and my way of saying, 'Good luck with your new life.'"

"What the—" Eddie began as Rosie opened up the envelope and pulled out a thick piece of paper.

As they both read it silently, she let out a small, "Oh, my!"

"What is it, for God's sake?" Mabel called out.

"It's a deed for a house," Eddie said.

"And a barn for animals on the property." Lon added, "So, Rosie, you can take in as many animals as you want. I've even hired a regular helper for you. Make it a real business, if you want."

"So now you have everything, it seems," Clara blurted out.

"Not quite," Eddie said. Approaching Beatrice, he stood before her, his face solemn. "Mrs. Paige, it would honor me if you would come live with us in Fillmore. Looks like we'll have plenty of room for you."

All eyes were riveted on the seamstress. Rosie held her breath, her trembling hand resting on her chest.

Beatrice paused for what seemed like forever. Finally, she spoke. "The name's Bea, Eddie. And I thought you'd never ask!"

THE END

THANK YOU

Thank you so much for taking the time to read *Trouble in Glamour Town*. I hope you enjoyed it. If you did enjoy reading it, I would certainly appreciate a short review on Amazon or Goodreads.

I would love to hear from you directly as well:

Please visit my website at https://www.srmallery.blog. Also, you might enjoy my history boards on Pinterest at www.pinterest.com/sarahmallery1.

ABOUT THE AUTHOR

S.R. Mallery, Gold Medalist winner of the 2016 READER'S FAVORITE Book Awards for Anthologies and 2017 READERS' FAVORITE Gold medal winner for Historical Personage, has been labeled nothing short of "eclectic." She has been a singer, a calligrapher, a quilt designer, and an ESL teacher. As a writer, history is her focus and is woven into her stories with a delicate thread.

Made in the USA
Monee, IL
01 September 2023

41990389R00121